DAY TRADING

A Detailed Beginner's Guide to Start to Day Trade for a Living with the Best Tools, Learning Risk Management and Trader Psychology to Generate Passive Income and Become Financially Free

By Andrew Clarke

Table of Contents

Introduction

Welcome to the world of daily trading! If you have this book in your hands, it means you are thinking of becoming a professional day trader and earning your living from it.

This book will help you learn A to Z of intraday trading. From the very basics to the complicated strategies and trading psychology, this book will explain everything in plain and simple language. It will act as a trading guide for beginners.

With this book, you can learn the important aspects of the day trading in a step-by-step manner and prepare yourself to be a day trader.

In financial markets, many types of entities are available for buying and selling. People use different trading styles to achieve their money-making goals from financial markets. There are long term traders, known as investors. Then, there are short-term traders, who use various forms of trading; such as swing, intraday, or even scalping which is done in time frames of one minute or less.

Day trading is a completely different ball game. It involves a lot of patience, preparation, and planning to become a successful day trader. This book aims to explain the necessary ingredients for mastering this skill. Yes, day trading is an acquired skill. Nobody is born a trader, nor can anyone become a successful day trader overnight. Like any other money-making venture, this activity is also a business. And like any other business; it also requires favorable conditions, money management, and risk-taking to earn profits.

If you are new to the day trading business, this book will act as your guide. It will show you the map, the way of reaching your goal of becoming a successful trader. This book will tell you where to start, which steps to take in the journey of day trading, and finally, how to train yourself so that you can become a successful trader.

I have written this book with a conviction that with practice, anybody can learn the skills of day trading. And, with just a little bit of self-discipline, anybody can become a successful trader, and start earning a side-income from it.

Please remember, you will not become a successful trader by just reading this book. You will have to practice the methods and tricks this book shows you about day trading.

When it comes to trading, our reaction to the market is more important than what happens in the markets. This is true for any venture, be it business or sports. The playing conditions are the same for everyone. Then how is it that one person achieves amazing success while many others fail to do so? It happens because that person's response to the playing conditions were more in sync than other persons. Similarly, financial markets are the same for everyone, but only one Warren Buffett achieves tremendous success, where many others have lost their fortunes.

This emphasizes that you can learn as much as you want. But ultimately, it will be your actions that determine the your success in day trading. If you are standing before a mirror, and you want the person in the mirror to raise its arms, what would you do? Would you force the person in the mirror to raise its arms? No. If you raise your arms, the person in the mirror will do the same! Your success in day trading will be a similar exercise, whether you are trading in forex, commodities, stocks, or options. Markets will open, trade, and close. But how you react to those market conditions, will define how successful you are in day trading.

CHAPTER 1:
Become a Successful Day Trader
And Earn Your Living by Day Trading!

What is Day Trading?

Before the advent of computers, only those people were involved in trading who had direct access to stock markets.

These were mostly from financial institutions, trading houses, or brokerage houses. Short-term trading was considered gambling; day trading was not popular in those days, and stock markets were meant only for long term investing.

Once the internet became accessible to common people, day trading or short-term trading also rose in popularity. Online trading and brokerage houses emerged quickly and attracted a large customer base. The convenience of accessing stock markets from one's home; or sitting in a cafe, created a new, lucrative career for or those who were interested in financial markets. Suddenly investors became an old-fashioned word, and day trading became the buzzword.

With the rising popularity and concept of making money by just sitting at a desk, came some misconceptions. Before we proceed further into the mechanism of daily trading, we must clear these misconceptions.

1) Day trading is NOT some get-rich-quick scheme:

The biggest fascination, and the misconception, about everyday trading, is that it is a money generating machine. It is not. People mistakenly assume that all you have to do is buy and sell every day, and you will be making big profits. This kind of thinking leads to huge losses for retail traders, who blindly jump into stock markets, listen to the advice of their friends, colleagues, TV experts, or even scamsters; and eventually lose their shirt. Trading in financial markets requires a thorough knowledge of the functioning of these entities, a disciplined approach, and considerable patience. Do not make the mistake of imagining day trading as easy as playing a lottery or gambling in the casinos. Money making, in any business, is not dependent on luck or chance. It is a calculated risk; which is taken after meticulous research of that field of business and knowledge. If you wish to enter the arena of day trading, make it your career, and earn your living by it; then learn its intricacies. Study all those aspects that impact the results of day trading. Take a step-by-step approach for acquiring the necessary skill sets to finally become a successful day trader.

After all, when you are spending money to earn money, you cannot afford to be unsuccessful in that venture.

2) Day trading is NOT a 9 to 5 job:

Another common misconception that causes loss for many retail traders, is, that day trading is like their 9-to-5 job. They assume; you start trading as soon as markets open, (reaching the workplace at a fixed time), trade through the day, and close your trades when the closing bell rings (leave the work workplace at a fixed hour). Workings of financial markets are not like a steady desk job. A plethora of factors affect the functioning of financial markets and their entities, such as stocks, commodities, currencies, and indices. These are all instruments of day trading and are influenced by the happenings in business, finance, and geopolitical events. There is a very common term related to trading. It is called "market volatility". This term denotes the fluctuation in financial markets. While there are hardly any "fluctuations" or rapid changes in any 9-to-5 desk job, in the world of trading fluctuations happen in seconds! This volatility can be stomach-churning for new traders. One can only master these volatile fluctuations in stock markets by having an in-depth knowledge of how markets function and learning to use this volatility for trading. Remember, when you begin day trading, you put your money at risk. Your purpose should be to obtain every bit of knowledge, which will decrease this risk and improve the chances of reward.

The Basic Concept of Day Trading

Day trading, or intraday trading in market parlance, involves the purchase and sale of any particular security in the financial markets within the same trading day. This kind of trading can happen in any market, but the bulk of day trading happens in the stock market or foreign exchange (forex) market. Because of geopolitical upheaval, nowadays commodities like oil and gold are also attracting a lot of intraday trading, but this book will focus on the most common securities for such trading, namely stocks.

Day trading is like investing, the only difference is, the time frame of buying and selling becomes very small in day trading. While investors buy a security for many years, even decades; for a day trader, the window between buying and selling is within the same trading session, and sometimes within a few minutes.

The difference between an investor and a day trader is because of their trading styles. Investors buy or sell any stock based on the fundamental analysis of that stock's company. They consider the long-term financial performance of the company for investing in its stocks. But day traders make decisions based on the technical analysis of any stock. This involves how the stork has been performing or trading for the last few hours or days. Investors look for steady and safe returns while day traders are more interested in small but quick profits. Investors follow the adage of "buy and hold". But for any day trader, the mantra is to "buy and sell".

As a community, day traders are usually those with disposable capital, and can 'invest' in the stock market for a very short period; usually for a single trading session. With the growing popularity of this trading, brokerage houses now provide margin facilities to encourage people to do intraday trading. This margin facility means, traders can buy or sell securities with a fraction of the total amount of that trade. The margin facilities offered by brokerage houses have brought day trading within the easy reach of those people, who can afford just a small amount of money for their daily trading activities.

For short-term trading, the most important thing is that the stock price should move quickly within a small period. The pace of change in the stock price is triggered by various factors, including news reports. Day traders keep themselves abreast of reports that can cause fluctuations in the market. Fluctuations, or volatility, are the best friend of day traders because it offers them chances to make quick profits within a few minutes or a few hours.

These fluctuations can be caused by a company's earnings; general elections; a change in the central banks' monetary policy; even trade disputes between countries like the US and China. These events can create a big churning in the stock markets within a few minutes or hours. Normally, commercial websites give breaking news, or financial calendars, with a list of such events that inform day traders about the possibility of what could happen in the markets. It is an important aspect of day trading and essential for any aspiring day trader to keep track of.

Short-term events are more important for day trading and their typical day is spent scanning news reports, going over the economic calendar, and watching companies' earnings schedules. They seek an opportunity to buy or sell based on these events. In a way, these changing conditions make day trading an exciting world. Market conditions change; breaking new changes; a hot stock from yesterday could be dumped by traders like a hot potato today. It is an ever-changing world. At the same time, it requires skillful maneuvers that come only with knowledge and practice. A day trader is constantly learning, both from mistakes and profitable moves; from news headlines to economic events. Day trading requires that one quickly adapts with the change in market conditions.

How Much One Can Earn by Day Trading?

The frequent question aspiring traders always ask is, how much money a day trader can earn? People who are trying to get into this field, whether they want to earn a side income or a livelihood, are disappointed when they do not get any definite answer to this question.

The reason is, the stock markets themselves are unstable entities. Stock markets function in a way, where the pattern of price movement changes every second. It can fall, or it can rise rapidly. In a business where conditions change with such a high frequency, it is difficult to anticipate how much profit one can make. Also, successful traders never publicly declare how much profit they make. All the information in the public domain is speculation by big traders. Similarly, brokerage houses also do not publish any data about how much profit day traders earn. Although they publish all the other data; such as the volume of trading; numbers of shares traded; numbers of traders in the markets; how many shares were purchased and how many were sold any day. However, nobody declares the profit-loss data of day traders. In public forums and chat websites, one can find traders discussing various trading strategies, some of them will accept that they lost or made profits. But again, it is all just chat and bravado. The real numbers are never divulged.

There is an adage in the stock market, that out of every 100 traders, 97 make losses and only three can secure profits. It is just a saying, but it shows that many day traders fail in stock markets. Yet, there is a small percentage of profitable traders. To get a place in this elusive group, the easiest way is to learn about stock trading and the stock market as much as one can. The success rate in the stock market depends on one's knowledge and psychology. If one has learned everything about trading and still fails in self-discipline and self-control during trading; the rate of failure will be higher. On the other hand, if someone is focused, is not emotional while trading, but lacks a substantial knowledge of how the stock markets function, then this person will also have a higher failure rate.

Many successful traders have written books about how they overcome their initial failures and finally succeeded in earning a living by day trading. They all suggest that these two points are necessary for steady success in stock trading. Steady success in trading means steady profits or income. How much income? That will depend on how much capital you invest in your day trading business.

For example, anyone who starts trading with a small capital of $30, will make smaller profits, compared to someone who is investing $3,000 in trading. Again, it must be emphasized that investing a bigger amount of trading capital does not always translate into profits. The higher number of transactions will also attract a higher cost of brokerage and a bigger rate of losses if the trades go wrong. Therefore; money management and risk management play an important role in how much a trader can earn by day trading. Successful traders always advise starting small and slowly building gains over time. The number of successful trades is the final criterion for earning profits in day trading. Suppose a person has invested $3,000 in stock trading and makes 50 trades a day. Out of those 49 are loss-making. Another person, who is trading with a small capital of $30, makes 10 trade in a day, and out of those, 9 are successful. The money invested is not important but successful trades will define the rate of success between these two traders.

In conclusion, it can be said that instead of focusing on profits, if you focus on trading right, then you can earn a steady income from day trading.

Traits of a Successful Day Trader

Two types of people trade in the stock market. Those who have lots of disposable money and spend their time trading as a hobby. They usually lose money in the markets. Then, there are professional traders, who earn their living by day trading. These are among the minority of successful traders. It is interesting to see what characteristics make them successful in trading, while the majority fails.

Professional traders are not set apart by any professional degree course. They stand tall among the crowd because of their trading traits. To become a successful day trader, it will be well to study their qualities and try to adopt the same habits.

A successful day trader spends time and money learning about the stock market; gathering knowledge of day-to-day events and news reports and is skilled in technical analysis. Fundamental analysis does not have any place in day trading. Technical analysis provides tools and guidance for short-term trading. Professional day traders are proficient in chart reading. Through the technical analysis of stock charts, they can anticipate how the price will move in various time frames such as daily, weekly, monthly, or even within an hour. Since day trading is limited to a single session which lasts from 5 to 6 hours, knowing how the price moves in different time frames are essential for successful trading. Professional day traders always study charts before they get ready for trading. This is how they plot their trade entry and exit points. In other words, professional traders always prepare their trades in advance. Others or novice day traders go by their "gut feeling" how the market will behave and lose their money because they trade with no knowledge.

The main characteristic of successful professional day traders is patience. The best traders can sit for hours, or days waiting for the right moment to trade. Amateur traders jump into the market as soon as the opening bell rings and start buying and selling. they trade first, then think. Professional day traders sit quietly, watching the price movements and create a trading pattern. Their trading decisions are based on the chart patterns, which show whether markets are tilting towards selling or getting support for buying.

Cautious money management is another trait of successful traders. They have sufficient capital for trading, which they handle carefully. When markets are not showing considerable price movement, successful traders stay out of big trading and put only a small portion of their capital in trades. They invest big amounts of trading capital when the stock price makes big moves in the market and the chances of profitability rise. Their priority is to keep their risk-reward ratio lower. This means they avoid unnecessary risk and trade only in favorable market-conditions to reap good rewards. Professional traders always keep strict stop-loss in their trades, to keep their losses to a minimum.

Another characteristic that defines a successful trader is preparation. Professional traders study markets and prepare a strategy of how to trade in different market conditions. They are always ready for changing market situations and change their strategy as the market-trend changes. All their trades are strategic and follow a certain trading plan. It is like searching for a treasure trove with the help of a map. They spend considerable time to study markets and prepare their trading strategies before they trade.

Successful traders are also very different in their approach to stock trading. They do not trade every day, but only when the price movement matches their strategy and trading plan. They plan and decide beforehand: in what market conditions they will trade; when they will exit the trade and book their profit; or sometimes, losses. They let their profits run and cut the losses quickly. They do not trade in anger, or greed, or fear. In simple words, they do not trade emotionally and always have a balanced and neutral outlook towards trading.

Day Trading to Earn a Living

Can one day trade for a living? The answer is; yes, one can.

Usually, people earn their livelihood in two ways. They can take a 9 to 5 regular job, or they can start their own business. Jobs usually have fixed working hours, and the income (salary) is also fixed. In jobs, everything is usually certain and regular. When you opt to run your own business, you put your money at risk; there are no fixed working hours you are working 24/7; there is a limited risk of losing your capital investments; profits are uncertain but could be unlimited.

Day trading is a combination of these two methods of earning a living. You market trade for fixed hours, so your working hours are also set like a regular job. But, like a business, you will have to invest money in this venture and a chance of losing your money or making unlimited profits will always be present.

It is possible to earn one's living by day trading. There are two avenues for this:

1) Become an individual trader, or

2) Work for financial institutions where you can trade for the company and its clients.

Those who work and trade for any institution or company, are called institutional traders. It is easy to make a living out of day trading as an institutional trader because the investment is from the company, you just trade on its behalf and receive a part of profits as your commissions. Apart from a fixed salary as an institutional trader, you will receive many technological and professional benefits; such as being part of a trading desk, access to sophisticated and latest charting and trading software, faster trading terminals, etc. The biggest advantage is, you will not have to put your own money at risk. You only have to use your reading skills to earn a profit for the company or its clients, and your commissions will be based on how much profit you can earn for the company.

Working as an institutional editor trader is a fixed job. You will trade only during the market hours; get weekends off; get all public holidays and your money will be safe from any untoward risk. You will get a fixed salary, and bonus as a commission from profits.

But most of the people want to become an individual trader. They seek freedom from the routines of an office-job and having a boss over their heads. They wish to do something, which has the potential of bringing them unlimited profits and being their own boss. Day trading gives people a vision of just sitting with their computers, buying and selling, and making bundles of profits, but this is not so. Day trading is a professional venture. You need to learn about the stock market, chart reading (technical analysis), keep abreast of happenings in the financial world, and learn the finer points of day trading. Even while trading, you need to be alert and cautious all the time as the price movement keeps changing every second.

Day trading is essentially putting your money into a venture, and then being on your toes all the time so you can quickly exit from any loss-making trade and make quick decisions if any of your trades are profitable. Remember, there are hundreds and thousands of institutional traders working on behalf of big hedge funds and banking institutions, with all the sophisticated technology at their fingertips, have professional training, and use all these advantages to make money. As an individual trader, you will have to compete with this vast group and your only asset will be yourself.

If you believe that you can learn a new skill, have the psychological strength of handling day-to-day pressures of changing market conditions, and have enough capital to survive on small profits initially; you can certainly think of becoming an individual trader and earn a living by day trading. You can adapt the conservative approach by starting small, then steadily growing your trading business.

As you start understanding how markets behave, what conditions are good for trading and what not, and how news affects stock markets; your trading will also improve. Slowly, you can start earning steady profits. Once you are comfortable with the initial trading, you can slowly increase the invested capital and look to increase your profits in small increments.

Should Day Trading Be Your Career?

Should you choose day trading as your career?

This depends on many factors. First; how much disposable income you have in-hand that you can safely invest in the stock markets (without putting your lifestyle at risk)? Second; how strong is your temperament? Like every other profession, day trading also requires some career skills. A doctor, an engineer, or a computer expert; they all go through different trainings. They choose their career based on what they enjoy doing and their temperament.

If you want to choose day trading as a career, you will have to look within and ask yourself a few questions. People, who are too impulsive or emotional, should not make this career choice. If they want to do so, they must undergo some emotional training by paper trading or by trading a demo account. This will help them learn to stay calm and composed during high volatility in stock markets. Such choppy times demand quick decisions within a split second. The biggest risk in day trading is emotional trading, which causes loss to most of the small traders.

Two emotions: fear and greed, are the biggest obstacle for any person trading in stock markets. If you have a position open and markets go against that position, you must take decisive action of exiting that trade. At such times, fear can make traders uncertain and they lose money by not taking the right decision. An opposite condition, when markets are going in favor of one's open positions, can also cause losses when greed takes over and traders do not exit their positions at the right time. Most of the time, traders lose money by not exiting markets when they are in a profitable stage. Eventually, markets change pace, those profits reduce but greed keeps trader immobile, and soon, their gains turn into a loss.

Learn to conquer your emotions and trade in a neutral state. If you are a person who prefers facts over emotions, it will be a helpful trait for performing well as a day trader. For short-tempered or egotistical people, the stock market can be a brutal eye-opener. Traders getting angry is a common sight in stock markets. Especially when markets do not go in their assumed direction. In anger, they keep trading against the market and keep losing their money. Similarly, some people make it an ego challenge that markets must go in their chosen direction. To prove their point, they keep betting against the market-trend and ultimately, incur losses.

While choosing day trading as your career, patience is another trait needed in a heavy dose. There are hours and days; sometimes even weeks when markets do not make any conclusive move. Trading in such conditions is usually a loss-making venture. Professional traders stay calm during such market conditions and stay away from trading. They wait for a big price movement, because profits and made only in those conditions. Retail traders or individual traders are in a hurry to earn money, so even if markets are not making any conclusive moves, small traders keep buying or selling. Because of the small price movement and directionless trend, they end up losing money instead of earning profits. This can be very irritating, and some people start to trade emotionally at such points; which leads to more losses.

Therefore; if you have extra money to invest in day trading, have the patience of sitting in front of the computer screen doing nothing but just watching markets, and if you believe that steady wins the race; day trading can be a suitable career for you.

Overview

With the arrival of the internet, a new form of trading has become very popular. It is called day trading or intraday trading, where people buy or sell stocks, currencies, or commodities within a single trading session. Before anyone decides to become a day trader, they must understand, it is not a get-rich-quick scheme, nor it is a 9 to 5 job where they can earn a fixed income. To earn profits from day trading, it is essential to have a good working knowledge of how stock markets function and what tools are essential for intraday trading.

The basic concept of day trading is like investing. The only difference being a shorter time frame for purchasing or selling any entity in financial markets. Day traders are not bothered about the fundamental analysis of any company, but they take the help of a technical analysis of stocks for short-term, intraday trading. With the ever-growing popularity of this type of trading, brokerage houses have started giving margin facilities where anyone can buy or sell stocks or any other security with a fraction of the actual cost of trading. For day traders, short-term events are very important; such as companies' earnings, or geopolitical events, which can trigger high volatility in stock markets.

People frequently ask about how much a day trader can earn. No certain data is available about that, but most of the people make losses and only a handful of traders are successful in earning money by day trading. Many successful traders have written books about their methods and they emphasize, that knowledge about stock markets and self-discipline are crucial if one wants to earn a living by day trading. Instead of focusing only on profits, if day traders focus on trading in the right way, they will be more successful in this field.

A few things separate successful traders from those, who miserably fail in stock markets. Those who succeed in day trading go about it professionally. They spend their time and money in learning and acquiring knowledge about trading. They also exhibit plenty of patience and wait for the right time to trade. The unsuccessful traders are impatient, and instead of knowledge-based trading, they believe in their gut feeling about markets. Successful traders also manage their money very carefully and are cautious about the risk and reward ratio of their trades. Before trading, such professional traders spend time in preparing a systematic plan and follow it.

There are many ways to earn a living by day trading. One can take at a job in any financial institution or a hedge fund, and trade on behalf of the company. One can also become an individual trader, invest one's own money, and earn a living by making profitable trades. Day trading is a combination of a regular job and business. Like a job, there are fixed market timings, but like a business, the money is also at risk in day trading. One can start day trading small and increase the invested capital over time when profits have become steady.

Day trading as a career is not for everyone. Impulsive and emotional people should stay away from this field because it can cause them financial losses. Those who make decisions based on facts and can stay calm and composed in stressful situations are more suitable for choosing a career in day trading. Emotions like greed and fear are the enemy of a day trader. Anyone who wants to be successful in this field should learn to control these emotions by going for paper trading or demo account trading first and start trading with the real money only after considerable experience of how to tackle volatile markets.

CHAPTER 2:
Learn to Become a Day Trader

The popularity of day trading started in the late 1990s, during the Dot-com bubble. For day traders, it was easy to book profits during those days; they did not need any skill. The stock markets used to make such big moments that it became easy to buy and sell internet stocks and make huge profits every day. That was a brief, but a very heady and profitable period for day traders, as they traded tech company stocks and made big money. The tech index NASDAQ was skyrocketing during that time, going up by thousands of points within a few months. Day trading was a booming business because it was a huge wave in the tech ocean, and traders were surfing on the back of that wave. Once the Dot-com bubble burst, and markets came back to their normal trading pattern, day trading also became less profitable. However; it remained a lucrative career for many people.

With the Dot-com era, online trading also saw rapid expansion. That brought day trading within the reach of common people. It made people realize, day trading was also a profession, like other professions, where one can achieve success with mastering the required knowledge and skill set. In day trading, one buys and sell stocks, or any other financial entity, through the day. For doing so they need to know various skills and tools, understand the right time to buy or sell stocks. Big financial companies cropped up overnight and started day trading on behalf of their clients. Banking institutions started opening their securities branches for common people, where they trained their clients to become skilled in trading.

Since then, the popularity of day trading as an income-producing vocation has been increasing. If you are looking to become a successful day trader, here are a few things that you will need to learn:

Knowledge about stock markets: As a day trader, have at least the basic knowledge of stock markets. You should know which stocks or companies are popular in the stock market. They will trade with higher volume, and volumes play an important part in day trading.

Basic principles of technical analysis: Unlike the fundamental analysis, the technical analysis tells how the price will move in a smaller timeframe, which is essential knowledge for day traders. So, if you are thinking about making day trading your career, this is a skill set that you must have. There are many online courses on technical analysis and chart reading. Various institutions also conduct offline workshops to teach this. You can join any of them and gain a basic knowledge of how to analyze charts, and what tools to use for day trading.

Money management skills: This goes without saying that you cannot spend an unlimited amount of money in stock trading. Before you start, you must set aside a fixed amount for your trading business and manage that money carefully. You should always know your losses and profits so you will understand how your trading business is going: successfully or failing miserably. You can find many books online about money management in day trading. Reading a few popular ones will give you a good idea of how to manage your risk and reward ratio.

Learn about trading psychology: Emotions are terrible for day trading, and you must have some knowledge about controlling your emotions during trading. Many successful day traders have written books about trading psychology. It will be a good idea to read a few of them before you trade. No business can survive on emotion, and before you enter the trading arena, you should be able to control your emotions; whether you make profits and losses.

What Differentiates a Day Trader?

Day traders are technical traders. They rely on chart readings for executing their trades and ignore any other thing like the company's profitability, P/E ratio, debt-to-equity ratio, etc. For a day trader, technical charts are the only tools for making money. Usually, day traders trade through a single session and by the close of the day, they also close all open trades, not keeping any position open for the next day. Traders who keep their position open for the next session or overnight, are swing traders.

A day trader can use many time frames on technical charts for trading. These time frames can range from one minute or lower to 5 minutes; 15 minutes; 30 minutes; 45 minutes; 1 hour; 4 hours; or even weekly and monthly. If you are wondering how day trader can use weekly or monthly charts, know the difference between using various time frames. Day traders decide their trading style by looking at the charts and deciding which time frame will suit them the most. Many day traders can spend hours in front of their computer screens every day. But several day traders trade only part-time, are busy with other jobs or work, and cannot spend much time for trading every day. In such situations, these traders can study weekly or monthly charts, and decide at what price level they will buy or sell any stock. After deciding that, they wait patiently for that level to arrive and trade only at then. There are many ways to set an alert to know when a price level has reached. The brokerage platforms have SMS facilities to alert their clients about stock prices. Mostly, charting software also has facilities to alert about a stock price level. By trading this way, they save precious time and money, which they can use for pursuing other money-making activities like a regular job or doing some other work.

There is another. highly skilled type of day trading, call scalping. This is also known as micro-trading because the day trader focuses on a small timeframe (such as one minute or a few seconds), and trades for tiny profits. They keep the lot sizes higher so that small profits will also multiply into big money. Since the timeframe is very small, scalpers can trade several times throughout the day, sometimes even 20 to 50 times. But this is a risky type of trading and requires very fine trading skills. Otherwise; one can end up losing all the trading money within a single session.

Day trading is also about buying and selling on the same day. But compared to scalping, day traders have a bigger time frame for keeping their positions open. This can range from minutes to hours. The Internet is full of articles that portray glamorous pictures of day trading, making you believe that you can get rich quickly by this trading method. But this trading method requires hard work, knowledge, razor-sharp focus and high levels of patience; not to mention a big chunk of money to invest in the early stages. If you are day trading, then you should be completely focused, you cannot allow yourself to be distracted by other things. If you can afford to have this kind of discipline and dedication, then you will find day trading suits you.

Another name for day trading is intraday trading. This term is a clearer definition of a day trader since it shows that buying and selling are happening within one day.

Day traders can develop their style into other types of trading such as momentum trading, positional trading, swing trading, or long-term trading. All these styles are specialization forms of trading, but usually, do not fall under the day trading category.

Part-Time, or Full-Time Day Trading?

For day trading you do not have to stay glued to your computer screen throughout the day. You can do part-time day trading or full-time.

As a full-time day trader, the best option will be to join any big financial institution as a day trader and work for them. This will ensure that you get a monthly salary, and perks, if you're performing well. This will suit you if you think of day trading as a hobby and do not wish to put your money at risk by trading. You will also benefit from the company's trading recommendations that are regularly sent to their clients. You can utilize them for your trading while doing the job.

On the other hand, you can opt to be a full-time individual day trader. Here you will have to do all your setup, invest your own money and rely on your skills and knowledge.

As an individual trader, you can also adopt a part-time trading routine, if you do not wish to let go of your stable job and jump into full time into day trading. All you have to do, is observe markets, find out which hours have a higher level of trading activity (or higher volumes), then trade only during those hours. For example, if you are looking for day trading in stock options and futures, the highest trading activity in these entities happens at the opening and closing hours of the stock market. Just prepare your trading strategies, and plan how you will trade (buy or sell). After that, you can trade only in the first hour of markets' opening, or the last hour of markets' closing. The price volatility is very high during these hours because big traders are opening or closing their positions and preparing for the next day. This makes the price move constantly and gives day traders a good chance to earn profits within that hour. Remember, the volatility levels will be very high during these hours, and you must be highly skilled and emotionally stable to tackle trading during this time frame. If you let emotions like fear and greed overpower you during these trading hours; chances are you will end up making wrong trades and suffering losses.

For those, who cannot day trade during the regular hours in stock markets, forex markets provide an excellent chance of trading through the 24 hours. Forex or currency markets function Monday to Friday, 24 hours a day, and close only on the weekend. This gives day traders unlimited access to trading through the week, and they can trade at the time most convenient for them. Because of this, forex trading is more popular than stock trading among day traders. Another thing that favors forex trading is the very technical nature of this trading. Anybody who has a basic knowledge of technical analysis, can trade in forex markets and be successful. There are different currency pairs that day traders can pick for trading. In forex markets also, the opening times of major regional markets provide higher levels of activity, which day traders can take advantage of. First among such active times is the opening in Asia markets, then the opening time of European stock markets and the highest level of activity in forex markets is seen when the US stock markets open. So, one can also become a part-time or full-time day trader in forex markets. For trading in forex markets, learning technical analysis is necessary. Knowing the schedule of important economic events is also essential because these events usually trigger extreme volatility in forex markets.

Things You Need to Start as a Day Trader

Apart from using your intelligence, there are some physical things that you will need to start your day trading business.

The most important thing is professional trading software and an internet connection of high speed. When you are starting at the beginner's level, one laptop will be enough for you. But as you gain expertise, and increasing your trading business, you will need a minimum of two monitors to check different charts and technical indicators. You will need multiple screens or monitors to watch the chart in different time frames because the price movement differs in these. To make the right trade entry or exit decisions, you will have to consider the trading pattern of major time frames.

Your trading platform will provide you with the market data that will help you in deciphering the price moments. It will be prudent to make sure you check the speed of this data. Live updates of these numbers will be essential for making the correct decision. Some brokers and trading platforms spend money on getting real-time data feed. But at times, smaller trading platforms provide a data feed that is delayed by a few seconds. That can make a crucial difference in the trading decisions. So, make sure, you trade with only reputable trading platforms, which provide a proper data feed to their customers and help make the right trading decision.

The internet connection for trading should be at a fast speed. To avoid interruptions, keep a secondary internet and power connection always ready if the primary ones are disrupted for any reason. Also, you may not think it necessary, but it will be well to keep the phone within your reach, so you can call your brokerage in an emergency. There are times when modern technology fails, and your brokerage platform may face some technical problem. In such situations, you may not be able to execute any order and then you will need the help of your brokerage house. Since seconds can make a big difference in day trading, it is always safe to be ready for any kind of emergency and keep the phone nearby.

The laptop or desktop used for day trading should also have a good memory and adequate speed processor. You wouldn't want it crashing in the middle of some important trading order.

You will need a day trading charting software to prepare day trading strategies and plan your trades in advance. Some brokers provide various charting software through which traders can plot the chart. Make sure that this software runs smoothly and provides essential options, such as various timeframes and technical indicators. Many charting software is available in the market, but make sure to purchase one that is suitable for day trading. Different software may have separate features suitable for different styles of trading. For example, if you want to try your hand at scalping, and the software you purchased supports only hourly timeframes, it will be useless because for scalping, one needs the charting capabilities of 1 minute and lower time frames.

You will also need to compare and select a suitable broker among the lot. Remember, you will have to pay brokerage or commission for every trade executed on their trading platforms. So, it makes sense to go for a broker that charges a low commission for trading. Carefully compare different brokers and opt for the one, which is reliable with its data feed, its customer policies and quick to return your money or profits.

Learn Technical Indicators

Technical indicators are tools to help traders in technical analysis of stock charts. For day trading, learning about how to use technical indicators is a very essential craft, without which you cannot become a successful day trader. This is like learning to ride a bicycle if you want to win medals in the competitive bicycling events. Fortunately, the technical indicators are simple and easy to learn, and anyone can find several online resources that explain what technical indicators are and how to use them.

You can also join some offline workshops or lessons to learn technical analysis. There are dozens of technical indicators used in isolation or combination by day traders. The good thing is, all technical indicators help in some way to spot the price movement and hint at the right trade entry and exit points. Day traders select technical indicators that they like and feel comfortable working with. It is possible to become enamored with too many technical indicators and try to use many of those for chart analysis. But the best practice is to use only a few indicators and stick with those for your trade analysis. Using too many indicators can create confusion and make your chart a jumble of crisscrossing lines. Keeping it simple is the best when it comes to using technical indicators.

Many traders depend on finding support or resistance levels for trading in stock markets. Support levels are favored for buying and resistance levels for selling. This is also known as buying low and selling high. These levels are the most important points you will need to know on charts for the right trading. Based on market trends, different methods are used for finding these levels. Mainly, there are three types of trends in the stock market: uptrend, downtrend, and sideways trend (also called range-bound trend). In the uptrend, the price continues to climb up; in the downtrend, the price falls regularly. But, in a sideways or range-bound trend, the price moves up and down within a horizontal range. In the up and downtrend, a slanting trend line shows the trading pattern. The Moving Averages are slanting indicators that move with the trend line and show major support and resistance areas. These indicators consist of different periods; such as the 20 days; 50 days; 100 days; and 200 days. Day traders use moving averages to find support and resistance points while markets are trending.

On the other hand; the sideways trend is created by a horizontal movement of price. In such trends, traders require knowing horizontal support and resistance levels for buying and selling purposes. Day traders use pivot levels or Fibonacci levels in range-bound market conditions for spotting support and resistance. These are the simplest of indicators. Pivot levels are calculated by certain methods and pivot calculators are freely available online. Fibonacci levels are drawn on technical charts from the highest and lowest price points. All trading charts provide facilities to draw Fibonacci levels.

The third most important and simplest trading indicator is the RSI (Relative Strength Index). As the name suggests, this indicator shows the strength of any trend. RSI is plotted below the main charting area and keeps rising and falling with the price moment. A rising RSI shows the strength of an uptrend and falling RSI shows the strength of a downtrend. It has the top and bottom areas, respectively called overbought and oversold areas. Day traders look to sell from the overbought region and buy near the oversold area.

One can combine support and resistance indicators with the RSI and plan their trading strategies for buying and selling.

Basic Day Trading Strategies

With the help of basic technical indicators, as discussed in the previous segment, you can create basic day trading strategies. Any day trading strategy has two parts. The first one will involve your preparations for trading, and the second one for interpreting how markets are behaving.

In your preparation, again there will be two sections. One will be related to money management, and risk and reward ratio planning. The second will involve chart reading and creating your trade entry and exit points based on the technical signals.

These technical signals will show how markets trade within that session.

Before you trade, decide how much money you will invest, how much loss you will allow if that trade goes against the planning, and what will be your profit booking point. Use technical indicators for analyzing the charts, and study how the price has been moving in the last few days, weeks, or months. By paying attention to the price movement in the recent past, you will get a fair idea of the trend in the stock market. Based on that trend, decide which technical indicators to use and prepare your trading strategy. For example, if you see on the chart that the trend has been up, or down, use moving averages to decide the trade entry point.

Using the same indicators, decide where you can safely book your profits and exit the trade. If you see a horizontal trading pattern on charts, it will show that the stock markets are trading in a sideways pattern and the price is range-bound. In this market condition, use the Fibonacci level and Pivot points to decide trade entry and exit points. You must remember that in a sideways trend, the price movement is restricted and thus, there is a risk of over-trading. Many professional traders completely avoid trading in the sideways markets. It will be a good trading strategy to follow this principle of not trading in a range-bound or sideways pattern.

For day traders, the best market conditions are when prices are in a trend. This can be an uptrend or downtrend. In such conditions, the price moves quickly with big volume and day traders can make healthy profits within a short period. Successful day traders wait for such market conditions and when the price hits the big trail, they are quick to follow its movement and trade steadily to earn money.

The best day trading strategy is, always follow the market's support and resistance levels. On technical charts, supports are areas where the price stop after falling and reverses. Similarly, resistance is an area on charts where the price pauses after rising and reverses. Therefore; traders look to buy near support levels and exit near resistance. This strategy can also be used in reverse order, where the trader sells near resistance and exits near the support level. Such a strategy is called "short selling" and is used by traders who have a negative outlook about the price movement.

Stocks, future and forex trading follow these basic strategies. However; if you are looking for day trading options, you will have to study very specific strategies used for options trading. One can trade in stock, forex or commodity options. These have a complicated system of calculating price movements, and beginners shouldn't go for options trading.

The final step of your basic day trading strategy will be to choose stock with high volumes or volatility. In other words, it would be a popular stock. Volume levels show that numerous traders are buying and selling that stock. So, its price will move in a quicker away. High volume stocks give day traders good opportunities to day trade it and earn some good money.

Remember Self-Discipline

During intraday trading, self-discipline can be your best friend. The lack of it can also be your worst enemy. If you do not have self-discipline or do not develop it before starting to trade, you cannot handle the roller coaster emotional ride of stock trading. All professional traders warn against the pitfalls of emotional trading: namely trading under the influence of greed and fear.

To become a successful day trader, one needs to develop a habit of self-discipline while trading. For this, successful traders advise beginners to start with paper trading or demo account trading. These are done in real-time with the help of real price moments and charts. Only the money is imaginary. The results of these "practice trading" help day traders learn how correct they are in trade execution.

It also helps them learn how stock markets behave from day to day; what causes volatility in markets; when they should trade and when they should stay away from it.

Successful day trading is mostly a result of habitual trading. Professional day traders develop a routine of trading. They follow the same routine of how they trade, how they exit their positions. And they follow it meticulously. Such traders usually look for a price pattern, which creates a profit-earning setup. Traders then create a trading strategy around this setup, identify which technical signals will show this trade, then trade only when this specific price pattern appears on charts. The rest of the time, they refrain from trading and just wait patiently for the right trading opportunity to come up. This routine trading behavior has many benefits. Their trading capital is safe, losses are minimum, and chances of profitability are maximum. It is the best example of discipline trading.

Beginners may find discipline management a tough thing to master. But this is the most crucial element in establishing a successful trading business. Your training routine must include pre-market analysis and changes during the market hours, as the price patterns develop. Once market close, have a post-market routine where you should analyze how the whole session went by. Always follow your trading routine, always do your preparation. And trade only when you have a trading plan in place. If, for any reason, you could not study markets before the opening bell, stay away from trading that day.

Create an analysis routine for the weekends, where you should study the weekly and monthly charts, check the economic calendar to know what economic events are scheduled for the next week and decide how you will trade during that time. Major economic reports or events like central bank meetings always trigger high volatility in stock markets. For beginners, it is better to stay away from trading during such times.

If you are a part-time trader, decide during which market hours you will trade, and stick to that schedule. Even as a full-time trader, try to not trade during lunch hours because the volume and price moment becomes slow-paced in that duration. This happens because hedge funds and financial institutions have a break from trading in that hour and since they make the biggest bulk of traders in stock markets, in their absence, the trading activity becomes lesser, and price moments slow down. Trading during the middle hours in markets is just wasting your time and money. Professional traders often say that knowing when not to trade is an essential mantra for success in the stock market. It will be good to remember this mantra for profitable day trading.

Always remember, it is you who can make or break your day trading career. Your actions will be responsible for profits and losses in stock trading. So, develop a disciplined version of you before starting to trade. It will stand you in good stead.

Day Trading Success

Before you dream of minting money from day trading, let's look at the success rate of day traders. As discussed previously, there is no data on how many day traders make money in the stock market, but it is estimated that only 10% of traders are profitable who trade intraday.

There is a long list of investors who have succeeded in stock markets, but there is no such list for day traders. Of course, there are successful day traders, but they keep quiet about their profits. Unlike the legendary investor Warren Buffett, no individual can say that he became a millionaire or billionaire by day trading. Those hedge funds or financial institutions that encourage retail traders for intraday trading, do not do so themselves. Their simple explanation is, day trading rewards are not enough to justify the financial risk.

Going by the data, if only 10% succeed in day trading, and 90% lose, then why people are so interested in this trading method? And, will anybody be able to earn a living by day trading? Again, the answer depends on the individual. With a professional mindset, knowledge, and self-discipline; yes, one can make a living by intraday trading. Like any other business or even professional sports, preparation is the key to successful trading. 90% of traders fail because they trade without requiring the skill set. They go by what TV anchors tell them, newspapers write, or other failed traders advise on chat forums. This is the reality. If a hundred people take part in the 800-meter race, and only one wins, it shows that the winner had better preparation and practice than the losers. There are hundreds of successful tennis players, dozens qualify every year for the US Open or Wimbledon tennis championships, but only one person wins. That does not mean the other players are not talented or capable of winning the championship. The difference is, the winner prepares in a better way.

Similarly, if 90 out of one hundred traders fail, that does not mean that you also will fail. Your success will always depend on your skills, temperament, and attitude towards day trading.

Those who make the mistake of thinking day trading is like a lottery and gambling will end up losing their money to those, who take this trading as a professional business and prepare likewise.

No business is easy. Day trading also is a business and it can provide a significant amount of earnings if you dedicate yourself to do it properly. Learning day trading needs time and money, just like any other professional skill. Steve Jobs and Bill Gates worked hard and faced obstacles before they tasted success in life. Day traders also face various obstacles before they can establish a trail of steady profits. Some give up, and some continue to improve and survive in this challenging field. Success comes to those who try to improve their trading methods, learn from their mistake and trade with a neutral mindset.

Developing a robust trading method will create the foundations of a successful day trading career. Learn as much as you can, observe markets, do paper trading or demo trading for the first six months, only then trade with the real money. Manage your trading capital astutely. All these factors will give you a professional edge in the day trading career. There is no reason that you cannot succeed where the majority fails. Your success rate in day trading will depend on how seriously and professionally you take it.

Overview

Day trading has become a highly popular activity, where people try to earn a side income or make a living by this method. To succeed in day trading, one has to have a basic knowledge of stock markets, technical analysis, money management skills, trading psychology. Unless you have a clear idea of these basic concepts, you cannot know how to trade, or what market conditions are suitable for day trading.

The basic difference between other traders and day traders depends on the trading style. Day traders base their trading on technical analysis. They do not go into the nitty-gritty of how any company is functioning. Their interest lies only in stocks and how it has been trading in the most recent past. Day trading can be of different types; such as scalping or momentum trading. A day trader leaves no overnight open position, or for more than a few hours.

One can become a full-time day trader or a part-time one. Full-time day trading can be done by taking a job with any financial institution, brokerage house, or individually. Working as a full-time day trader with any financial company has its advantages. Individual day traders must rely on themselves for setting up the trading business. Part-time day trading suites those who already have a full-time job and cannot spend much time watching stock markets.

To start day trading, one needs a few essential things like professional trading software, high-speed internet connection, opening a trading account from where trades are executed, backup for internet and power resources, etc. While selecting a trading broker, one must consider how much commission it charges, because this will have a big effect on trading profits or losses.

For a successful day trading, learning technical analysis is a must. Some basic technical indicators are usually good enough to spot the market trend, deciding trade entry, and exit points.

Support and resistance levels are very helpful in day trading. These levels can be deciphered with the help of technical indicators; such as moving averages, Fibonacci levels or pivot points. There are many books and online lessons available to teach technical analysis. One can also join offline courses, workshops, or classes to learn it.

With the help of technical indicators and analysis, you can create basic day trading strategies. Money management and risk analysis should be a part of these strategies. By chart reading and with the help of technical indicators, you can also prepare the trade starting and trade exit points. Day traders plot different strategies to trade different trends, such as an uptrend, downtrend, or sideways trend. It is advisable to not trade during the sideways trend, or when markets are range-bound.

Self-discipline plays a very important role in successful day trading. Day traders can develop self-discipline by paper or demo trading before they invest money in stock markets. Emotional trading causes big losses to day traders. By learning not to trade in emotional states like fear or greed, day traders can eliminate a lot of risk from their trading style. Successful day trading depends on a stable trading routine, which involves preparing a plan before trading.

The day trading success rate is usually very low, but that happens because day traders jump into markets without proper information or preparation. Day trading can be a source of steady income if one takes it seriously and prepares like a professional trader. For this, it is necessary to develop trading skills, gather knowledge about stock markets and their functioning, and form a robust trading method. Success in day trading depends on the trader, and not on any outside factor.

CHAPTER 3:
Preparation for Day Trading

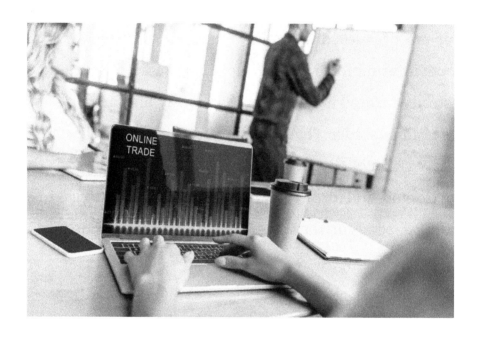

All over the world, stock markets open in the morning. Those day traders who think they can start trading while munching on their breakfast, with no preparation, are among those who make losses. All businesses open in the morning. No successful businessman just gets up, yawns and starts his business activities. Successful professionals arrive in their office with a clear idea of how they will tackle the work and related challenges. Likewise, to succeed in day trading, one must prepare beforehand. These preparations include many aspects; such as mental, physical, emotional, and financial.

Professional traders have clear advice for day traders; never trade if you are tired or stressed; never trade if you are feeling highly emotional, and trade with clear money management concepts. Day trading is a sophisticated business activity, where people try to earn money by using their intelligence. Therefore, physical or emotional stress can cause harm to your trading business. You will not be able to make rational decisions if you are tired or feeling stressed.

Before you start the day's trading, you should be physically, mentally and emotionally alert. A good night's sleep is necessary for traders to tackle the roller coaster ride of stock markets. Here are a few steps that will help you prepare for day trading with a cool temperament and calm mind.

Before going to sleep, keep your trading plan ready. Check the stock chart, make notes on the chart what big patterns the price created in the previous session. Note down the important support and resistance levels. Then mentally go over this chart and imagine how you will trade in the next session, in different trend conditions.

Do not spend too much time watching news about stock markets or anything else. Watching the news may create doubts in your mind about stock trends and influence your decision-making power for the next session. If possible, do some breathing exercises or meditation before going to sleep, which will sharpen your focusing power and reduce stress.

Also, prepare your money-plans for the next trading session. How much you will invest? What will be your loss tolerance level? And, what will be your profit booking point? During the trading hours, these decisions have to be made in a split second, and if you are already prepared, you will not hesitate to make the right decision. These will also help you set your goals for intraday trading. Just stick to your goals and you will not face any decision-making problems during the trading hours.

The final stage of your preparation will be an hour before the markets open in the morning. This is the time when you check the news reports about the business and financial world, and the economic calendar. By doing so, you will know what events could influence that day's trading pattern in the stock market. You can also check how the world markets are trading in that session. Sometimes all markets trade in one direction, which will be beneficial to know before your local stock markets open.

Planning for Trading

In day trading, financial instruments are bought and sold within the same session. Sometimes more than once through the same day. To be successful in this endeavor, traders need to know where the price might make important moves. Technical charts are very helpful tools in deciphering this price moment. Anybody involved in stock trading relies heavily on stock charts, which is why successful traders always create their trading plans before making any trading decisions.

When you create a trading plan, you are creating an 'assistant' to help you during the trading hours. This assistant will have all the information you will need for day trading; such as trade entry, trade exit, profit booking, stop loss and major price moments. Nobody goes looking for a treasure trove without any map. Likewise; no trader worth his or her salt will trade without a trading plan. Let us look at how a trading plan is created:

A trading plan is based on research, takes time, but saves a lot of effort and precious money during the trading hours. It is one of the most essential tools required for success in day trading. Every day trader has heard this saying 'fail to plan, and plan to fail'. Professional traders don't tire of emphasizing the importance of a trading plan. If you take their advice and prepare a trading plan before the markets open, you are halfway through to successful trading.

A trading plan is prepared before markets open and so, it is open to revisions and changes after markets start to trade and price changes. Every trader has a different trading style and based on that his trading plan could differ from others. But every trading plan must have a few essential details. These are:

1. Major support and resistance levels: One must mark the major support and resistance levels on the trading chart because these will symbolize the trade entry and exit

points. These levels should be visible on charts to help in decision making during the chaotic trading hours.

2. Trade entry rules: Your trading plan should include when and why you will enter a trade. This could be a detailed explanation like 'if the price goes above X level, then buy'. Or it could be just a green arrow pointing to that price level.

3. Trade exit rules: Like the trade entry point, mark a trade exit or profit booking points on your trading plan. You must follow these rules meticulously, otherwise, these will become useless, if you plan and do not follow them.

4. Money management rules: Some traders like to note down on their trading plan, how much money they will invest in the next session. They keep checking their profits and losses through the session, and if the day's loss reaches its threshold; they stop trading. This is a good example of money discipline while trading because, in the excitement of trading, one can lose sight of what is happening with the investment capital.

These are the most basic rules to include in the trading plan. As you gain experience and get a hold of trading patterns in stock markets, you can expand your trading plans and include more trading rules in it. But always remember, these rules must be followed. A trading plan is based on research about markets, so every rule is important. Breaking any rule will be like going against the market, which is always harmful to any trader.

Chart Reading & Candlestick Charts

Day traders use different charts for technical analysis. The main types are line charts, bar charts, and candlestick charts. Some Forex traders also use Heiken Ashi and Ranko charts, but candlestick charts remain the most favorite of traders. The reason for this popularity is its simplicity. A green candlestick shows a positive price movement, and a red candlestick signals a fall in price. Day traders use various candlestick patterns to decipher the market trend.

The candlestick charts are more than a hundred years old. These were first used by Japanese rice traders to document the rise and fall in the rice prices. It was such an accurate system that stock traders also adopted it and it has since been a popular chart creating tool.

A single candlestick has two main parts; a body and a tail or wick. The body of the candlestick shows the opening and closing levels, while the wick shows the high and low marks. A green body shows that the price opened low but closed higher. And a red body shows higher open, but lower closing in that time frame. A single candlestick can be assigned to different time frames, ranging from one second to one month. These candlesticks make various patterns on charts. Traders try to decipher the price moment by how long the wick, or the body is, and how every candlestick is placed with other nearby candlesticks.

Candlestick charts are also used for automatic or algorithm trading, where buy and sell signals are generated by various patterns formed by candlesticks.

The up and down movement in stock prices creates candlesticks on charts. Sometimes, a single candlestick can indicate a trend reversal from high to low or low to high. These are called engulfing candlesticks and are so large that they completely engulf the previous candlestick. These can be both bullish and bearish candlesticks. A bullish candlestick is formed when the price-move creates a big positive or green candlestick, which overshadows the previous one. It signals that the price is ready to move higher and to start an uptrend.

Its opposite is a bearish engulfing candlestick pattern. Here, the stock price makes a big red candlestick overshadowing the previous one. This signals big selling pressure and shows that the price will fall further.

Another popular form of a candlestick is "Doji". Usually, this candlestick forms near the top or the bottom, after the price has made a long moment in either direction. In a Doji candlestick, the body is tiny, and the wicks are long. A small body denotes uncertainty in buyers and sellers; which shows that the market cannot decide whether to go up or down. Such an uncertain signal on top may indicate a trend reversal, and traders prepare for a fall in the market. A Doji formation at the bottom signals that the downtrend may come to an end and traders look for confirmation of a price-rise from lower levels.

Candlesticks create many types of patterns on a technical chart. This could involve a single or two or more candlesticks. There are many books about candlesticks and how to read candlestick charts. Traders who wish to know more about these charts, can read some of those books and enhance their knowledge.

Manage Your Time Effectively

Day trading is a demanding profession and requires significant time. Any market session runs for at least 6 hours a day, and you will have to spend that much time watching and observing markets; even if not reading. Apart from trading hours, a day trader needs to research, create trading plans, and keep learning new things. All these require time and effort.

Therefore; to succeed in day trading, you will need to manage your time effectively. Usually, people want to adopt a day trading career so they will have working flexibility. This means freedom from getting up early and rushing to get caught in the morning traffic, freedom from having a boss, and of course, financial freedom. Nothing comes easy in this world. A dream life also requires putting in lots of effort. Many day traders find it difficult to complete their trading routines; such as after-hours research and planning. Part-time traders who are already busy with some other work also struggle to prepare for day trading in their spare time.

With just a few adjustments, a day trader can find enough time to complete all steps required for a successful day trading. Here are a few things you will find helpful in managing your time effectively, while day trading:

1. **Healthy sleeping hours**: day trading can be a mentally exhausting activity. Watching the computer screen for 6 hours a day, then reading news reports, preparing charts-all these tires our brains and eyes. This is the reason day traders must have at least 6 hours of sleep during the weekdays. TV watching or being glued to your smartphone can increase stress on your eyes and make you feel more strained. For a successful career in day trading, you should sacrifice these low-value activities.

2. **Fix targets**: the human brain is most active when it is given a target to achieve. So, create reasonable monthly or weekly targets in your day trading. Challenge yourself to achieve these goals with self-discipline. For example, set a target of trading only twice in a session, for a week. This will be an indirect way of managing your money and reducing the risk of over-trading.

3. **Prioritize your tasks**: fix times for different tasks such as trade planning, charting and going through the economic data and news. For day trading, you need to do all these activities regularly. Assign time and prioritize which one is the most important and do that activity first. For example, trade planning is the most essential tool for successful day trading but reading news items are not that important. So, give priority to planning your trades first.

4. **Relax**: It is of utmost importance that day traders relax over the weekend when markets are closed. Some traders keep going over news reports, chatting in forums about what will happen in the markets next week.

However; it is essential to take time off from trading and relax. Day trading is a stressful vocation and too much stress can burn anyone out. Shut down your computers once market close for the day and relax for an hour or two before picking up your trade planning activities. Likewise, over the weekend, when markets are closed for two days, it is essential that one unwinds and enjoys the free time away from markets and trading.

Start Small

Believe it or not, the biggest stumbling block for day traders is the beginning. They jump into stock markets and start trading heavily, thinking of making big money instantly. This is their first and the costliest mistake. The functioning of stock markets is always very chaotic.

From a calm morning, the opening of the stock markets is like rushing into the path of an express train. When stock markets open for trade, day traders have to make split-second decisions, monitor the technical signals, keep an eye on the price movement, think one step ahead of markets, and take care of trade entry and exit points. All of these things happen together. In such situations, it is difficult for day traders, especially beginners, to make mistakes. Therefore, day traders should initially keep their trading restricted. They should focus only on one or two stocks, and trade only once or twice through a single day.

Starting small is also important for your risk and reward ratio management. Even if you stumble in the earlier stages of your career, you will keep the losses to a minimum by trading less. Day trading is like learning to ride a bicycle where initially you will often fall. But once you get used to it, you will learn how to balance it. In day trading also, it is advisable to watch and observe stock markets for the first few days. Prepare your trading plans, then watch how the price moves with the signals. Slowly you will start getting the hang of the seemingly chaotic behavior of stock markets, and a definite pattern will start to emerge. This pattern will show you where to start your trading and where to exit.

Many brokers have now started giving facility of margin trading, where day traders can trade with a fraction of the required money. For example, if Apple shares are trading at $200, day traders are given the margin facility of trading it for a smaller margin of, say, $20. On the surface, it is a win-win situation for the broker and the client. It increases the business for the broker; and gives day traders facility to invest very little money for trading. But the margin facility can also become a trap for day traders by encouraging them to trade more. It gives them a false sense of having more money to trade. That's why intraday traders must make a rule of trading only once or twice in the initial days and stick to this rule.

Apart from the invested money and the number of trades; day traders should also keep their profit target small. It is easy to make profits if markets are in a big trend. Then day traders start dreaming of making millions every day. This makes them greedy and they invest more and more money; trade many times a day; hope to catch a trend again. In stock markets that does not happen often, and they end up losing money instead of making profits. Always keep your profit targets small and achievable. Accumulate your profits, which will become big over a period

Pay Attention to Money Management

Like any other business, day trading also needs careful money management. As a day trader, you will invest a certain capital for trading, and you must keep track of profit and losses. You should always know how your business is doing. You cannot keep on investing money, hoping to become profitable someday.

The first step in money management during day trading is to decide how much you are going to invest in every single trade. After that, decide what will be your stop loss. This means, at what level of loss you will exit that trade. Before trading, you must make a mental note of how many trades you will do that session and keep that number to a minimum. Fix how much loss you will allow on all your trades in that session. For example, if you are thinking of doing two trades that day, and you can tolerate $10 loss for each of those, you should stop trading once your loss reaches $20. Such discipline in trading is crucial if you don't want to run out of your investment money within a few days of trading. This is not pessimistic thinking that all your trades will make losses, but a prudent money management skill, where you decide the limit of the loss you will tolerate.

When it comes to money management, most of the day traders fail because they focus too much on analysis and planning, not about how they will utilize their investment capital. This happens because of an outward outlook on day trading. Traders are so focused on markets; they do not focus on themselves. Every trader knows that money management is essential for success in day trading, but like exercise and dieting, money management also remains that elusive thing that everybody talks about, but hardly anybody practices.

Your success in day trading will depend on money management as much as your trade planning and preparation. For earning money from stock trading, a disciplined approach to investing your money will be the best gift you can give yourself for your trading business. All successful businessmen always focus on the profit-and-loss ratio. Your day trading business should be no different.

If a majority of day traders fail in stock markets; it is because of the lack of money management. They are eager to count their imaginary profits but ignore to keep track of their real losses.

To handle your investment money carefully, break it into chunks. First, invest only one chunk in your initial trades and keep the rest of the money as surplus. Then it will be easy to know if your trading is profitable or loss-making. If that chunk of money grows; your trades are making profits, and if that first chunk of money shrinks, it will show that you are incurring losses. If your trades are profitable, take out the profits and keep reinvesting the original amount. This way, you will be able to protect your profits. Some day traders become greedy and think, if they reinvest their profits, they will make even more profits. That is one sure way of making losses.

Stay Away from Penny Stocks

As the name suggests, penny stocks can be bought and sold for a few pennies. This makes them a lucrative day trading opportunity for traders, who are looking to start their business with a small amount. But these stocks are like a death trap for day traders because they are mostly illiquid. This makes it difficult to sell them if and when you need to. These stocks are traded over the counter (OTC), not on any major exchange. Several penny stocks that trade under $1 per share, attract day traders with low investment money. Some of these stocks are thrown out and delisted by big stock exchanges because of their company's dubious business practices. Sometimes, there are genuine penny stocks, but most of the time, these are just scams.

The internet is full of articles praising penny stocks, painting a glamorous picture of how one can trade these with low investment, and make money. If trading penny stocks were that easy and gave high returns, every day trader would be trading those instead of going after stocks of established companies like Apple and Google.

For a successful day trading, the selected stocks must have high liquidity. This means a high number of traders are buying and selling that stock regularly, which facilities a steady price-change in that stock. Penny stocks rarely have much liquidity and see sudden jumps or drops in their prices. If you are holding numerous penny stocks, and its price suddenly goes down, you may get stuck in a situation where no buyers will come forward to purchase that stock. Then you will be left holding a bundle of stocks rapidly losing their value, but you will not be able to get rid of those.

In the last few years, penny stocks have become very popular among traders who do not wish to invest bigger capital in stock trading. These stocks belong to the companies that have a much lower market capitalization. As a result, the SEC (Securities and Exchange Commission) identifies their stocks with a price range staying below $5 per share. Compared to blue-chip company stocks that cost hundreds of dollars for trading, penny stocks seem attractive for their low prices. But there is a reason they come cheap, and blue-chip company stocks cost so much. Their trading capacity. For every share of a blue-chip company, there will be hundreds of traders eager to buy or sell it. If you are trading in a blue-chip company's stock, you can do so within seconds. But penny stocks have a risk of trading with no price movement, and low trading volumes for a long time.

Trying to trade in penny stocks is mostly like trying to grow plants on a stone. You can put the seed on the stone and wait patiently for years but nothing will germinate. Sometimes it feels, only traders with insider information can be successful in trading these rocks. Therefore, if you want to save and protect your money, stay away from trading penny stocks.

Overview

Day trading needs a lot of preparation. If you jump into day trading without preparing yourself mentally, emotionally, and physically first, you will put yourself at risk for losses. Trading, when you are physically tired or mentally stressed, is not advisable. A day trader should be mentally alert and well-rested before getting into the trading business. Preparing a trading plan is also necessary for success in trading.

Preparation for trading has two main stages; one after markets close, and the second before markets open.

Day traders base their trading style on technical analysis. They do not care how a company is performing financially but watch how that company's stock trades over a few days. Intraday trading also includes scalping, which is called micro-trading because traders target small profits and trade in many lots. A day trader can broaden the trading style into different types; such as momentum trading, positional trading, etc.

For technical analysis, traders use different charts; such as a line chart, bar charts, candlestick charts. Of these, the candlestick charts are the most popular among day traders. Candlesticks are easy to interpret and create various patterns on charts that show how a trend is developing or ending. Day traders can easily identify these patterns and trade profitably. Many books on candlestick charts are available online, one can read these for comprehensive knowledge.

Day trading requires a lot of time and for any day trader, time management should take priority. Nothing comes easy in this world and those who are seeking a career in day trading to achieve financial freedom; should utilize their time well. Both for trading and relaxing. Spending too much, or too little time on stock analysis is harmful. Day traders should have a balanced outlook on the trading business.

At the beginning of a day trading career, traders should take small steps. Instead of trading too much and dreaming of making heavy profits, they should keep realistic goals and trade only once or twice in a session. They should start trading in small lots, targeting small profits. These can accumulate into big profits over a period.

Another thing they should focus on is money management. Just like any other business activity, day trading also needs astute money management. If you keep making losses and do not keep track of these, you will soon run out of your investment capital. Day traders should keep track of their profit-and-loss ratio and manage their investments carefully.

Day traders should avoid trading penny stocks as these are very illiquid and can trap your trading capital. Some day traders may find the low prices of these stocks attractive for buying and selling but trading a liquid and expensive stock is always advisable then trading in cheap and illiquid stocks. There are many articles on the internet praising penny stocks and painting a rosy picture of how day traders can make money from these stocks. However; traders should stay away from these stocks and remember; everything that glitters is not gold.

CHAPTER 4:
Online Trading Tools & Platforms

You will need to accept the help of some outside 'forces' to succeed in day trading business. Apart from your efforts, three things will decide if you can succeed or not at earning profits from day trading. These are trading platforms, charting software, and brokerage services.

Day trading was made popular by the electronic trading systems, also known as online trading platforms. These are computer software programs, for placing buy and sell orders for different financial products. On online trading platforms, the speed of data feeds and fast execution of orders have made them very popular with day traders. This is one of the reasons why many people now prefer to become individual day traders and conduct their business from any place, especially from their homes.

This is in stark contrast to traditional trading which usually happens on stock exchange floors where brokers yell on telephones and clients find it hard to get their desired trades executed immediately.

Electronic trading platforms also have another advantage. These relay live market prices to the clients' computer screen, which traders can use to decide whether they want to buy, or sell, or hold their positions.

Apart from an online trading platform, day traders also need to have sophisticated trading tools; such as charting software; account management tools; and newsfeed. In today's technology-driven age, one cannot imagine indulging in day trading with no charting software.

This software help in technical analysis of stock prices, based on which, traders take to buy and sell decisions. Automatic or algorithmic trading is rapidly expanding. Big traders use automatic charting software to generate trading signals that are automatically executed on their behalf.

According to their trading styles, traders have different requirements. Trading software is also based on various trading styles. For day traders, the speed of execution and tools for chart analysis are very important. Brokerage houses provide trading platforms that fulfill these requirements and attract many day traders as their customers. Some other companies have nothing to do with brokerage services but provide standalone charting software of excellent quality.

The third essential requirement for day trading is selecting a good broker, who provides competitive brokerage rates. With every trade, day traders have to pay some fees to the broker, which is called brokerage or commission. Since day traders usually trade in every session and mostly execute more than one trade every day, they need a brokerage plan where the trading commission is at a minimum. Take it this way; as the trading commission, traders incur a financial loss as soon as they place a trade, with every trade. Every trade has two legs; one buys and one sell. The brokerage is charged on both legs. To keep this money-outflow to a minimum, traders need a broker, who provides them necessary day trading facilities but does not charge hefty fees for this.

All these things; online trading platform, charting software, and broker's commission; will also constitute parts of your investment in day trading business. You will need to research and compare various services and tools, before taking a final decision. Once you invest money in these "parts" of the business, it will not be easy to change.

Introduction to Trading Platforms

Trading platforms are technical tools created with computer software. These platforms are used for trade execution and managing open positions in the stock markets. Online platforms range from a basic screen to sophisticated and complex systems. The simple and basic trading platforms usually provide only order entry facilities, not much beyond that. Advanced trading terminals have many other facilities, such as streaming quotes, newsfeed, and charting facilities.

Day traders should consider their needs while selecting a trading platform. For example, are they at a beginner's level or professional? No need to spend money on highly sophisticated platforms, when you are just beginning your day trading career. Different trading platforms are tailored to suit different markets: such as stocks, forex, commodities, options, and futures.

Based on their features, trading platforms can be divided into categories of commercial platforms and crop platforms. For day traders and retail investors, commercial platforms are more useful. These are easy to use and have many valuable features. On these platforms, day traders will find the news feed and technical charts good for day trading. Investors can use research and education related tools. Prop trading platforms are more sophisticated and are customized for large brokerage houses, who wish to provide a unique trading experience to their clients.

For beginners, it is advisable to go for some basic online trading platform that provides a simple and easy-to-understand interface. In the beginning of the day trading career, it will be difficult to adjust to the market volatility and learn new things with every trade. On top of that, any complicated trading program may confuse a novice day trader and cause losses instead of providing ease of business.

Day traders should consider two factors before choosing a trading platform; its price and available features. A live data feed is a must for any good platform. At the same time, it should not cost the moon and some more. Therefore, the day trader will have to balance between the price and trading features. Going for a cheap platform may help cut costs, but it could provide delayed data which will destroy your day trading business. On the other hand, a fancy trading platform will put a hole in your pocket and confuse you during trading by its overwhelming range of features.

Those, who day trade in options, will need different charting features than those who trade in stocks. Similarly; day traders in forex markets will need different types of trading platforms. Carefully consider what tools are available on any online platform. If that suits your requirements and budget, make a final decision to purchase it.

Some trading platform are available only for those, who have an account with a broker. Some may have high deposit rates before allowing traders to use it. It is also possible that some online trading platforms will easily give margin facility to their customers; while others may not provide it. All these things should be considered before investing into any trading platform.

Before making a choice, it will be better if you make a list of your requirements, then check that list against the features of any platform. Purchase the one that fulfills all or most of your requirements.

Day Trading Software

Many day traders use computer software for automated trading. This takes away their headache of spotting the trend and deciding the trade entry and exit points. Also, they need not spend hours on chart analysis and reading economic news to understand what will happen in stock markets. Day trading software takes care of all their time consuming and decision-making problems.

These days, trading software automatically analyze chart signals, decide trade entry and exit points, profit booking and stop-loss levels, and execute the trade on behalf of the trader. The biggest advantage of automated trading is, it takes away the hazards of emotional trading. Not everyone can control their emotions, especially in stock markets, where fear and greed overcome day traders. Under the influence of emotions, they do not spot the right trend and make trading mistakes. This is one of the very common mistakes in day trading, and most of the day traders who suffer losses, do so because they cannot control their emotions.

In such situations, automated trading software solves the problem by taking emotions out of day trading. As machines, trading software can only focus on facts and make trading decisions based on technical signals. These signals are generated by automatic chart analysis. Thus, the human error component is completely eliminated from machine trading. Automatic trading is also known as algorithmic (or algo) trading because trade signals are generated based on specific algorithms. Some traders prefer their customize algo-trading programs, where trade signals are generated based on specific signals.

Different types of automated trading programs are available nowadays. The simplest type of such program is standalone websites that provide trade signals for time-based subscriptions. These websites display trading charts, where real-time prices run through the session and generate intraday buy and sell signals. Day traders have to watch these signals and manually trade on their own trading platform. Such programs cost little, and day traders can continue their subscription, or discontinuous it, based on how much profit they make from it.

Some brokerage firms also provide automated trading programs to their clients. These programs run only on that company's trading platform, and day traders can directly place buy and sell orders from the program.

Big companies, hedge funds, and some individual traders are more inclined to use expensive algo-trading software, where everything is handled by the software itself; selecting the right trade entry, placing the order and exiting the trade at the right moment. Traders can also place advance buy orders. These get executed automatically when the price reaches that specific level. Likewise, they can place advance orders for selling a stock, at a specific price level, and the order is executed automatically at that level.

Algo-trading is blamed for increasing the volatility in stock markets. Big orders are placed near certain price levels, and when the price reaches that level, a sudden increase in buying or selling activity can create a stampede of panic in stock markets. This is especially harmful to individual day traders, who manually place their orders. The sudden churning in the stock market hits their stop loss levels before they can protect their position or understand what is happening in markets.

Choosing a Suitable Broker

In the day trading business, a brokerage service will be like your business partner, which will link you with the stock exchanges and give you a platform to execute your trade. Also, this service will demand a fee from you for every executed trade. Therefore, you will have to consider many points before you choose a broker for day trading.

A high brokerage can create setbacks in your profit-making efforts, and a low brokerage may hide some low-quality features of the trading platform. Since this brokerage service will be the medium through which you will execute your day trading business; compare different services before making your choice.

The first thing to consider will be; does the broker fit your needs? If you are going to focus only on day trading, then you must choose a service where the brokerage will be affordable for you. Check its features whether they are suitable for intraday trading or not. Choosing the right broker will be the first step in investing in your trading business. Investing in the right tools and services will provide a solid foundation for trading.

Different brokers cater to different trading and investing needs. Their tools and features are also tailored according to their customers' needs. A brokerage service, which is focused on long-term investors, may not be a good fit for day traders. In day trading also, there are various services that are tailormade for day traders of forex markets, some other target day traders in commodities markets. For day trading in stocks, you will have to focus on brokers that have the most comprehensive features for stock traders.

The second most important step in finalizing a broker will be its trading fees and facilities. As a day trader, you will be placing more trades every day. Therefore, low brokerage will suit your needs. Also, look for margin facilities for intraday traders, which will help you at a fraction of the original cost of trading.

Check out the broker's trading platform. Does it provide a live data feed of markets; or, is there any delay in its price feed? For a day trader, going for a trading platform with a delayed price feed will be like committing hara-kiri. Getting the right price at the right time is a must for making correct trade decisions. Also, the broker's trading platform should have good speed and should not face connectivity problems. Check out social media forums to know what other customers of the broker say about its services.

As a beginner, it will be better to go with a simple brokerage plan that fulfills your basic day trading needs. In the initial stages, you will have to focus on learning how stock markets function, and how to trade correctly. Once you have successfully established your day trading business, and feel confident about various trading tricks, you can think of upgrading your system and go for more advanced trading platforms and charting software.

Remember, tools and services can help you only up to a limit. Your biggest trading accessory will be your knowledge and skills that will help you establish a good day trading business.

Practice by Paper Day Trading

Everything can be learned with practice. Even the most difficult skills in the world can be mastered with regular practice. Sportspersons and actors are the best examples of what can be achieved by rehearsals. Day trading also sounds like an easy skill, but the reality is, once you trade, you will feel like standing in a cross-section where many freight trains will come at you from different directions.

Since day trading can cause a loss of a significant amount of money, it is advisable that day traders start with paper trading first, and upgrade to trading with real money once they become comfortable with the pace of stock markets.

In paper trading, everything else is real except money. Here, day traders see the real price charts, the real market data, and decide how they will trade without risking any real money. This is a sort of simulated trading, where day traders get to do real trades with fake money. This gives them a chance to learn from their mistakes, strengthened day trading techniques, and become familiar with stock market movements. This is just like actors rehearsing scenes before the real shoot begins.

Many brokers and online platforms offer demo or paper trading accounts to traders, where they can practice day trading for many months. It also gives them a chance to polish their chart analysis and money management skills.

It will be better to practice paper trading or demo trading with the same broker, with whom you plan to do the real trading. Using the same trading platform for paper trading will give you time to learn its features; practice order placing and using chart analysis tools. Therefore, when you will start the real trading, you will hit the ground running and will be comfortable placing your orders instead of searching how to execute a trade. Remember to check the price-feed in the paper trading facility. It should provide live market-feed for paper trading, so that the whole experience is real. To be able to do paper trading, or use the demo account, one will have to open a real account with the company providing these facilities.

One can also practice trading with the help of a live chart, without opening an account. This involves creating real trading plans, doing chart analysis, and preparing trade entry and exit points, fixing profit booking and stop loss level for the next session. When markets open, just follow your trading plan and mark on the chart where you will enter a trade and where you will exit. Mark where you will book your profits and where your stop loss will be. Follow all the steps you will during real trading, but do not place the real trade. Keep watching markets and observing the stock price. Write the results of your trading. Was it successful? If not, what went wrong? Did you rightly interpret the trade signals? If not, what were your mistakes? After the session closes, and you plan for the next day, check your notes and results of your mental trading. Learn from your mistakes and prepare a trading plan for the next session. Continue to do this mental trading for a few weeks. You will realize that your mistakes are becoming less, and your familiarity with market movements is increasing. This will give you the confidence to start real trading.

Overview:

In the day trading business you will need to use the help of some tools and services. Day trading has now evolved into a completely computer-based and online activity. It is starkly different from the earlier era of traditional trading where brokers used to yell on the trading floor and customers found it difficult to place a trade order. Day trading was difficult in those days. But the invention of computers and Internet has made day trading a popular activity, and individual traders now sit in the comforts of their home to trade easily.

To execute trade, you will need to use a trading platform. These are technical platforms that use computer software to facilitate trading. There are many types of such platforms that provide wide-ranging features. Some have a simple, basic screen for trade execution; while others have complex systems with many sophisticated features. Day traders should choose a trading platform as per their needs and budget. For beginners, it will be better to go for a basic online trading platform. Different trading methods requires trading platforms with different features. Some brokers provide specialized platforms to their clients.

Automated trading has become very popular nowadays. Many day traders prefer to use automated trading since it eliminates the emotional component from day trading. This is very beneficial when it comes to taking right decisions. Automatic trading software is based on certain algorithms. Trading with such software is called algo trading and is responsible for creating higher levels of volatility in stock markets. Automated software creates buy and sell trading signal, which day traders can follow manually, or allow the software to execute trades by itself. There are also standalone websites that provides trading signals. Day traders can purchase subscription of these websites and use their signals for trading.

For day trading, opening a trading account with some broker is required. These brokers act as the link between the trader and the stock exchanges. They also provide trading platform to traders. One should consider various factors while choosing a broker for trading. The most important things for selecting a broker are the brokerage commission and facilities provided on the trading platform. Day traders trade multiple times in a day, so they should choose a broker with lower fees or commissions. The broker must provide real-time market data; otherwise it can impact the trading decisions.

For novice day traders, it is always advisable to start with paper or demo trading. In such trading methods, except the money, everything else related to trading is real; such as real price feed, real chart analysis etc. It is like simulated trading, where day traders get exposure to real market conditions and trade realistically without putting real money at risk. Stock trading, particularly day trading, can be an overwhelming experience, especially when markets are very volatile. Paper trading helps day traders learn how to cope with such conditions, causing no financial harm to them. Beginners can also do mental trading where they can plot their trades on stock charts and watch if their trades go right or wrong.

CHAPTER 5:
Understanding Trading Orders

As a trader, you will need a broker through whom you will place buy or sell orders for any asset. You can decide whether you are going to buy or sell any stock, then place an order accordingly on your online trading platform.

Usually, exchanges use a bid and ask process for fulfilling orders placed by traders. This means that there must be a buyer and seller to complete a single order, and they both should agree on the price. For example, if a trader wants to buy a stock at X price, there must be a seller willing to sell that stock at the same price. No transaction can occur unless a buyer and a seller agree at the same price.

The bid is the highest price a trader is willing to pay to buy an asset, and the ask is the lowest price, that trader is willing to accept to sell that asset. In stock markets, the price moment is directed by a tussle between the bid and ask prices. These prices keep constantly changing. As trading orders get filled, the price levels also keep changing, which is reflected in the technical charts.

While day trading, one must keep in mind this bid and ask process, because this will determine at what price the order will be executed. When markets are moving slowly, the change in price is also slow and one can wait to get the trading orders filled at the desired price. However; when markets are highly volatile and sees big up or down moves happen within split seconds, the order may get filled on a higher than expected rate. This can cause losses to day traders as the price changes quickly and can reverse by the time their orders are filled.

Different markets have different methods of matching buyers' and sellers' prices. These methods are called trading mechanisms. There are two main types of trading mechanisms; order-driven, and quote driven. In markets that use quote driven trading, a constant stream of prices (quotes) is available to traders. These prices are decided by market makers, therefore; these types of trading systems are better suited for over the counter (OTC) markets or dealers. There is a considerable spread between the bid and ask prices, which constitutes the profit of the deal maker or the market maker.

Exchanges mostly adopt the order-driven trading mechanism. Here, orders are executed when buy orders match with a sell order. In this type of trading mechanism, dealmakers are not involved.

Mechanism of Trading Orders

In the electronic day trading, orders are placed on the online trading platforms. These orders are the trader's instructions to the broker, or the brokerage firm, for buying or selling some security. When you are trading stocks, you place orders to buy or sell a stock, which is fulfilled by the brokerage firm with whom you have a trading account. The ease of electronic trading has given traders the freedom to initiate various types of order, where they can use different restrictions in order conditions. By these restrictions, traders can control the price and time of order execution. Such instructions help increase traders' profits or restrict the losses.

In systems, where the trading mechanism is order-driven, traders can also control the timeline of any specific order. For example, a trader can place an order which will remain open until its execution. Traders can also place orders that last till the end of the session, or one day, or a specific time.

Understanding how trading orders are placed, and how they can impact one's day trading, is important because it can affect once profit or loss in day trading. For example, a novice day trader may not be aware of the slippage between the bid and ask prices. There is always a difference between the bid and ask price is called slippage. It occurs in every trade, and every trader faces it whether buying, selling, entering a position or exiting from a position. This is also called the spread between a bid and ask price. So, when you place an order to buy a stock at $4, the slippage may increase its cost to $4.05 when your order is filled. Likewise; when you are existing any position, you place an order to sell at $3, but the slippage causes it to get filled at $2.98, thus chipping away at some of your profits.

Professional traders advise beginners to stay away from highly volatile market situations because the slippage risk increases during those choppy moments. For example; on a central bank policy declaration day, stock prices become highly volatile and move with big numbers within seconds. In such a situation, the ordered price and executed price may be different, causing financial harm to the day trader. From the outside, such big moves may look tempting to day traders and make them greedy, thinking they can make big profits with such huge price moves. But the reality is, the slippage between the bid and ask price is equally big and it can change considerably by the time the trading order gets filled, or immediately after the order is executed, creating a loss-making situation for the trader.

Different Types of Trading Orders

Most individual traders use a broker or dealers' trading platforms to place their trading orders. These platforms provide the facility of placing various types of orders, which are helpful in trade planning. Placing an order on the trading platforms is instructing the brokerage firm to buy or sell a financial asset on behalf of the trader. Based on the execution type, here are some common order types:

Market Orders: These orders do not have any specific price. A market order is an instruction to the broker to complete the trade at the available price. Because there is no fixed price, these orders almost always get executed, unless there is some liquidity problem. Traders use market orders when they want their trades executed quickly and they are not bothered about the execution price.

These orders are good if there is not much slippage between the bid and ask price. But a big slippage can cause loss to the traders, especially those who day trade in options.

Limit Orders: Traders place limit orders when they want to buy or sell stocks (or other assets) at a specific price. For example, if Apple shares are trading at $220, and traders expect the price to dip low, they can place a limit order to buy the shares at $219 or lower. Limit orders can be used for both buying and selling. Traders use these orders when they are trading with technical levels and are sure of price touching those level. For example, if a trader has bought Apple shares at $220, and thinks it can touch $222, he can place a limit order to sell his shares at that higher price. When the share price reaches that level, his sell order will get executed.

Stop Orders: These are also known as stop-loss orders and make a part of traders' money management techniques. A stop-loss order can stop the trade from going below a specific price, thus restricting losses for the trader. These orders are used for both buy and sell trades. The price specified in a stop-loss order is called stop price; and once that price is reached, the order is executed as a market order.

Day Order: This order Is valid only in the same trading session where it is placed. If the specified price is not achieved by the end of the session, the order is automatically canceled. This saves day traders from carrying forward their orders to the next day.

Preparations for Placing an Order

When preparing day trading plans and strategies, many day traders forget to pay attention that how they will place orders for trades. Believe it or not, the simple act of placing a trading order can have a big impact on the success of your day trading business.

Successful day traders always give importance to order processing techniques and plan their trades around the stock price they will focus during the trading. The trading plan itself means planning at what price you will enter a trade and when you will exit. Online trading platforms provide many methods of placing your orders around your planned trade prices. You can prepare charts of your trade, mark entry, and exit points and place orders for both trades together, or separately.

A good trading plan always includes trade entry, exit, profit booking, and loss stopping points. The margin trading facility provided by various brokerage firms also includes placing a stop-loss order together with the primary buy or sell order. This ensures that your trade will never suffer a loss beyond a specific price level. Here is an example to illustrate this:

Suppose a trader has bought stock 'A' at $10. He is expecting the price to go up, so he'll make some profit. However; anything can happen in stock markets and in case the price reverses, he wants to restrict his losses to $3 only. So, he will place a stop-loss order at $7, which is $3 below his buying price. If the price keeps moving up, the stop loss order will remain inactive. In case, the stock price falls, nothing will happen till it reaches $7, at which time the stop loss order will be triggered, and automatically sell the stock he has bought.

A stop-loss order makes sure that even if the trader is not available to check prices, his position will be safe till a certain price.

Similarly, traders can also use limit orders to exit their positions after earning a profit. Taking the above example once again, if a trader has bought a stock at $10, and believes that the price will move up to $15; he can place a limit order to sell at $15. When the price reaches his target ($15), it will be automatically executed, and the position will be squared off with a profit of $5.

These examples show that day traders can use a combination of different order types for money management and managing the risk and reward ratio. By technical analysis of any stock chart, day traders can find at what price the stock will make a big move, and be ready to place their orders near that price level.

Some Other Order Types:

Apart from the basic orders, some other order types are not so common but can be used for money management or specific trading strategies.

For example, some day traders are more active during the market closing hours, as they create trading strategies for the next session. To take advantage of the price movement during the closing hours, they can place 'Limit-On-Close' (LOC) orders. As the name shows, it is a limit order and is specified for getting executed when markets close. As you know, a limit order controls at what price any security will be bought or sold. LOC has an extra parameter of 'on close', which adds another condition to this order, that it should only get executed if the closing price matches the order's price limit. For this order, both the limit price and the market's closing price are important.

Expert day traders use this order to take advantage of the closing time volatility in the stock markets, where they expect the price to reach a certain level. The LOC order has a drawback;

if the closing price does not reach the limit price of the order, it is not executed. Also, this order must be placed within a specific time, before markets close for the day. The LOC order is valid only through the same trading session and is not carried forward to the next session.

Sometimes when the trader places this order but its requirements are not met for a while, the trader decides to wait till it gets executed. In that situation, it will be called an open order. The order will remain open until the trader does not actively cancel it. All open day orders get canceled automatically at the end of the session. During the session. If traders do not wish to wait further for the trade to take place, they will have to cancel all open orders manually. The open orders are often caused by buying or sell limit orders or stop orders. Traders can use GTC (good till canceled) option for their open orders, which will carry forward their orders until it is executed. Traders have the option to cancel the open order at any time.

When traders open any order and then decide not to get it executed, they can cancel it and it becomes a canceled order.

This can happen when they mistakenly place a wrong order and upon realizing their mistake, immediately cancel the order. Or sometimes, they place a limit order, wait for it to get executed, then decide not to complete the trade and cancel the order. Market orders usually get immediately executed, so it is difficult to cancel a market order after it has been placed. But limit and stop orders have a time gap before getting executed. Therefore; traders can cancel these orders before their execution.

Overview

For stock trading, one needs to place buy or sell orders through a broker. There must be a buyer and seller to complete any order and they should agree on a specific price to complete the trade. Stock prices move through a process of the bid and ask. Day traders must keep this in mind when they are placing an order because the difference between the bid and ask price can cause slippage, which is harmful to a day traders' profits. Different markets have a different trading mechanism.

Online trading platforms facilitate order execution. Traders place their orders through the platform, which is executed by the brokerage firm. The time and method of order placing can impact one's day trading profits and losses. The spread or the difference between the bid and ask price can change at what price any trade is executed. Therefore; beginner day traders should stay away from volatile markets because, in those market conditions, the slippages can cause them considerable financial harm.

Day traders can use different order types to execute the trade. Market orders are executed almost immediately at the latest available price. These orders are good to use when markets are trending. Most of the time, day traders prefer to place limit orders where they can control the buy or sell price of their trades. Traders also used stop-orders to control the loss or to decide the profit booking levels in their trades. For intraday trading, traders can use the day order, which, if not fulfilled, gets canceled at the end of the session.

Order placing has an important place in traders' money management and trading strategies. Traders can pre-plan their trades and decide at what level they will buy or sell any stock. Technical analysis can help them find levels where the stock price will make considerable moments. They can place different orders near these price levels to manage their trades. Day traders can combine various orders to manage their risk and reward ratio.

Apart from the basic order types, there are many other orders, which expert traders use for their trading strategies. LOC or 'Limit-On-Close' Is one such order that traders can use to buy or sell stocks at the market-closing price. They can use this order type to take advantage of the closing hours' high volatility in markets, or if they are planning any strategy for the next day's opening session. Any order that is not filled is called an open order. Sometimes traders cancel their orders for various reasons, and these are called canceled orders.

CHAPTER 6:
Day Trading Strategy & Analysis

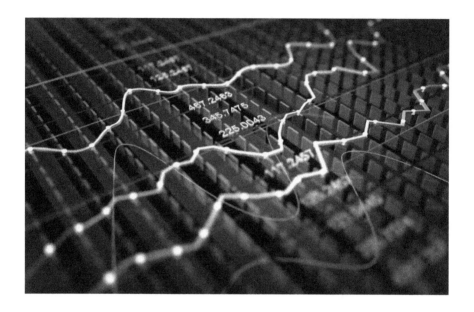

Now that the internet and the online trading platforms have made day trading easy for common people, many people think of adopting this as their career choice. There is a misconception among such people that with day trading, they can make easy money. In fact, day trading requires hard work; successful day traders spend hours preparing their trading strategies and doing chart analysis. If you are willing to follow their path, then you too can create a career in day trading.

Your success in this field depends on how you prepare your strategies, and how well you can analyze stock charts. For beginners, it can be challenging initially, but once they get to know the right way of analyzing charts and preparing trading plans, it becomes easy to prepare for day trading.

First comes the technical analysis of stock charts, based on which, trading plans and trading strategies are prepared. Technical analysis is done with the help of many technical indicators. These indicators are used to plot the course of price over various time frames. Based on how the price creates different patterns on technical charts, day traders expect how the price will move in the future. Accordingly, they prepare trade strategies; where they will buy or sell any stock; where they will put a stop loss or book their profits.

For day traders, technical analysis is the most important weapon in their arsenal. Since day trading is done within one session of 6 hours, traders must know how the price will move within that short period. If they don't know whether the price will go up or down in the next session, they will cluelessly buy and sell, incurring financial losses and brokerage.

Once they have prepared charts; day traders prepare their trading strategies based on the expected price moment. A wide range of strategies is available that can be used for day trading. Traders, who day trade in Options, need specialized trading techniques, which is beyond this book. About Options trading, many books are available online, which day traders can read to learn this specialized skill.

The most common strategy for day traders is buying and selling near support and resistance levels. These levels are marked on technical charts and day traders make buying or selling decisions accordingly. Learning technical analysis, creating trading plans and strategies is essential for successful day trading. The internet is full of articles and books about technical analysis and day trading strategies. It is advisable that beginner day traders spend some time learning and getting familiar with these techniques before they trade.

Trading Strategies for Beginners

There are many day trading strategies used by traders. Some of these are conventional, some unconventional; developed by individual day traders. These strategies include different forms of trading and using different technical indicators to find trade entry and exit points.

Scalping is a popular day trading strategy among Forex traders. Here, they trade for a very short time, looking to make small gains but accumulate them through the session.

Some day traders trade by market timings; referring to making use of the opening and closing hours' volatility.

Then there are range traders, who trade when markets are in a sideways trend and move within a definite, horizontal price range. Such traders make use of support and resistance levels to buy at support and sell at resistance (also known as buy low, sell high strategy).

Some traders swear by the importance of news reports, and they trade only on those days when some news report creates a big moment in stock markets.

Nowadays high-frequency trading has become popular where mathematical algorithms used to create trading strategies.

Since there are hundreds and thousands of day traders in stock markets, trading every day, developing one's trading strategy or using the established once becomes essential for success in day trading. With the help of hundreds of technical indicators and various trend theories, individual traders can develop their trading style and strategies. There are different trends in markets and different strategies are used to trade during those times. Based on the trend, these can be directional and non-directional trading strategies.

Directional trading strategies are used when markets are trending in the up or down direction. Trading with the trend line is the simplest directional trading strategy in trending markets. Trending markets can be bullish or bearish. Day traders use different directional strategies for bullish or bearish trends. For example, in a bullish market, day traders try to spot 'higher low' patterns and buy when prices create such a pattern. In a bearish market, day traders locate "lower high" price pattern and sell when such a pattern is formed on technical charts.

Non-directional trading strategies are simple to create because the market creates a series of highs and lows in a sideways trend. Traders draw a horizontal line linking all high points, and one line linking all lows. Then they sell when the price reaches the high-points' line and buy when the price touches the low-points' line.

Markets keep changing trends from time to time. The traders must spot the right trend and use the right strategy for profitable trading. Otherwise, they will only suffer losses. For example, their directional strategy may be correct. However; if they use it in non-directional markets; it will fail and cause them financial loss.

Select and Trade Only a Few Stocks

Your choice of stocks for trading should be aligned with your profit goals in day trading. Different traders have different investment capacities, and based on that, they choose their day trading styles and stocks. Traders who can invest heavy capital, prefer to day trade futures because trading in futures requires a big margin.

Those who are not willing to deposit big money, and, are looking to trade with a small trading capital, opt for intraday trading in options. There is an in-between category of traders, who buy and sell stocks in cash markets and look to generate profit from the intraday price movement.

Whatever may be your trading style, it is very essential to choose the right stock for trading. Stock exchanges create different categories for stocks of various sectors. So, you will have stocks of all financial companies in one sector and all technology stocks in another. These different sectors also have their separate indexes and have their trading patterns. You will have to do some research about which sectors are moving quickly, then which stocks in that sector have higher liquidity and trading volume. Select just one or two stocks from that sector and focus on them for trading.

Many day traders make the mistake of running after any stock that is making news that day and trade new stocks every day. This is a very fickle trading method and stops them from learning and analyzing the price pattern. This shows a herd mentality; to go where the crowd is going.

Successful day traders carefully choose a few highly liquid stocks, and trade only those stocks, ignoring all others. By doing so, they can fully focus on the analysis of those stocks, which gives them time to become familiar with the trading pattern of a few selected stocks. Stock markets repeat the price patterns at intervals. Therefore, any stock will have its particular support and resistance levels, which it will repeat in its trading pattern. If you follow one stock for many days, weeks or months, become familiar with its trading patterns, it will become easy for you to decide when to buy and sell that stock.

There are thousands of stocks available for trading in stock markets. It is easy to become tempted to buy and sell news-making stocks. But remember, it takes time to know any stock's trading pattern. Unless you are familiar with the price pattern of any stock, you cannot make correct trading decisions about that. Volatility is another criterion for selecting stocks for day trading. Highly volatile stocks are preferred for day trading because the quick fluctuations in its price give day traders a chance to profit from those price movements.

Follow Important Trading Rules

Day trading is not some half hazard activity, but a very systematic and planned method of trading stocks. If you want to become a successful day trader, always remember a few rules and follow them for profitable trading.

The first rule is to always plan your trades. Like cooking a dish. You don't just randomly throw some ingredients together, put them in a cooking pan and create tasty dishes ready to eat. There is always a method and planning involved in cooking.

Likewise; all businesses need planning for success, and day trading is no exception.

So, make it a habit of preparing your trading plan the night before. When markets open, you should be ready with a plan of buying, selling, putting a stop-loss, and profit booking levels for that day. The best day trading plan will fail if you don't follow it. Meticulously follow your trading plan, and soon, you will start accumulating profits.

Many day traders who want to leave their 9 to 5 jobs have a misconception about day trading. They assume, this is also a regular hours' job, where they trade for a few hours and earn their salary. If you treat day trading as a job, you will fail. To succeed in day trading, you must treat it as a business. In a job, you do not invest any money. But in business, you invest your own money and try to earn a profit from it. Always remember the rule of treating day trading as a business venture.

When you are investing money in some venture, like in day trading, it becomes your responsibility to protect your money. In day trading also, you must use all rules of money and risk management so that your money is safe. While trading, never leave your positions open without a stop-loss. All professional traders stress this point for a successful day trading. Putting a stop-loss saves your trade from losing money in highly volatile market situations. Another rule of money management is avoiding over-trading.

Always keep count of how many times you have traded in a day because every trade will cost you brokerage.

Another important rule of money management is, investing only the money you can afford to lose. If you have $200 and can afford to lose only $20, then put only that much money in day trading. Never borrow money for trading. Day trading is a business and therefore; here returns are not guaranteed within a fixed period. Never be greedy in intraday trading. Keep small profit targets and exit your trade once you have achieved your targets.

Follow these simple rules for safe and profitable day trading.

Profit-making by Short Selling

When people hear 'day trading', they think of buying stocks; making some profits; and then selling them. But selling first is another method of profitable trading. In trading language, it is called short selling.

Traders indulge in short selling when they have a negative outlook on markets and think the stock prices are going to decline. Short selling is an advanced technique and is not suitable for everyone. Once you have become an experienced day trader; you can start experimenting with short selling in declining markets.

Investors use short selling as a hedging technique to protect the investment in the stock market. When they have big positions open in stocks and some news or political event causes a sudden drop in stock prices, investors short sell an equal number of stocks, as in their portfolio, to hedge the loss.

Short selling is a risky technique; therefore, exchanges demand a bigger margin from traders. Mostly, futures and options see more short selling. These instruments have a fixed expiration time, So, traders are more likely to bet on a decline in these instruments within that period. However; if the price starts to rise against their short positions, traders can suffer big losses.

Short selling is not done randomly, but it is a well-thought-out investment or trading strategy. The strategy depends on the decline in price. Investors or traders anticipate this decline and short sell any financial security. The amount of decline in that security becomes their profit. Therefore; a rise in that security's price becomes their loss.

One cannot sell shares that one does not own, so for short selling, traders technically borrow shares from the broker or dealer, sell these in open markets, and buy shares when they want to book profit or stop the losses. This is the reverse process of more common buying first and selling later. In simple terms, short selling happens when a trader or investors open a trade by first selling some shares, then buying those shares again to complete the trade. Selling at a high price and buying at a low price makes up a profitable short selling trade.

Short selling can only be done with a margin account. Traders, who have open short positions, must pay interest on these and fulfill margin calls in case there is a margin shortage. Sometimes cartels short sell a company's shares for deliberately bringing down prices and harm that company financially. To stop speculators and gamblers from harming any company's stock prices, this process is highly regulated by exchanges.

Overview

Day trading has become very popular and easily accessible because of the widespread expansion of the Internet and online trading facilities. Many people think of adopting day trading as a career. But some people have a misconception that this is an easy money-churning activity. A successful day trading business requires lots of hard work, preparation, study, and money management skills. Day traders need to learn technical analysis of stock charts so they can prepare their trading strategy. Trading without proper analysis and strategy will be like throwing stones in the darkness and expecting to hit the jackpot.

Day traders can take advantage of many available day trading strategies. These strategies include various forms of trading and using technical indicators for spotting the right buying and selling opportunities. Common day trading strategies included scalping, range trading, trading on news reports and high-frequency trading. Intraday trading strategies can be directional and non-directional. Directional strategies take advantage of any strong movement in stock markets in up or down directions. Non-directional trading strategies are used when markets are in a sideways trend. For successful day trading, it is essential to spot the trend correctly; and apply the right trading strategy.

Stock selection for trading has a big impact on profitable day trading. Those who trade in too many stocks, do not get time to study properly or become familiar with their price moments. This can cause financial losses. For profitable day trading, it is essential to focus only on a few stocks, study them over the long-term and learn their price patterns. This makes it easy to spot buying and selling points in the trading pattern of that stock. Highly volatile stocks are good for day trading because the changing price moments give many trading chances to day traders.

 Successful day traders have trading rules and follow these rules strictly. Creating a trading plan is the first rule of a profitable day trading. If you are not prepared, you cannot read successfully. Day trading is a business, do not confuse it with a job. Money management should be an important rule of your day trading preparations. If you do not pay attention to your profit-and-loss ratio and do not take steps to protect your money during trading, you will soon be out of this business.

Short selling is another profit-making technique of day trading. This is used by investors and traders for hedging open positions or earning profits. Traders and investors use this technique when they have a negative outlook on markets and expect stock prices to decline. This technique needs enough experience in stock markets, so beginners should not try to short sell early in the day trading career. Short selling is also risky, and traders need to deposit bigger margins if they want to use this trading method.

CHAPTER 7:
Money & Risk Management Techniques

For successful trading in the stock markets, money management and risk management are crucial steps. Stock markets can turn highly volatile at times, and if you are not careful about protecting your money and risk of open trades, you can suffer huge monetary losses.

Therefore, the first step in day trading should be; learn how to reduce trading risk and manage your capital investment so you can tolerate the normal losses in day trading. Money management is like strengthening your defenses so you can survive in the stock market to trade another day. Safe trading practices to protect your money can increase your profits. A lack of it can also double your losses. Money and risk management can be the difference between success and failure of a day trader. Often, beginners are so focused on making profits in stock markets, they forget to protect their invested capital and soon; their losses wipe out the whole trading capital.

"A penny saved is a penny earned" perfectly explains the money management principle in stock trading. Often, day traders stay in a loss-making trade, thinking soon the losses will stop and the trend will reverse to award them profits. This is the biggest mistake they can do. It is always safer to exit a loss-making trade with a small loss and protect your capital from being wiped out completely. Putting a stop loss in all your trades is the safest way of protecting your trading capital.

Part of good money management is using just a fraction of your trading capital on one trade. In other words, never put all your money on a single trade. As they say, 90% traders do not make profits in day trading. A big reason for this failure is not paying attention to money management. If you keep on betting on stock prices for rising of falling with no proper strategy and risk management, then it is pure gambling and not any intelligent business venture.

Take day trading as a business, do it with proper money management, learn how you can reduce the risk in your trades; and you will reduce the number of potential losses and increase potential profits. Keep your trading cost to a minimum. Before opening any trade, always decide how much loss you will allow for that trade and put a stop loss to cover that much amount. Markets will come back the next day, but you should be left with enough capital to trade when markets open for the next session.

Understanding Margin Trading

Brokerage firms and financial institutions that allow day trading on their platforms, provide margin facility to their clients to trade stocks or other financial assets at a fraction of the original cost. This called margin trading, and it is usually restricted to intraday trade.

With the margin facility, a trader with $20 can trade a share that costs $200. Trading on margin is borrowing funds from the brokerage firm, and trading on that borrowed money for far many times then your money will allow, is not a good idea.

Margin trading allows day traders to trade multiple times in a session with a small investing capital. For prudent day traders, it is a good facility that they use for their profits. But for beginners, it may turn into a trap, making them greedy and losing money by over-trading. Margin facility gives a false sense to day traders of having more money than they have. During trading, they forget that they're trading on borrowed money and sometimes, accumulate more losses. Also, the brokerage charges pile up and total losses for them become higher than the money in the account. In such situations, traders get a call from their brokerage, demanding to deposit money in their accounts to cover the deficit. This is knowns as the "margin call' is and is a signal that the trader is accumulated losses.

Like nuclear power, margin trading can be good in experienced hands and destructive in the hands of novice traders who become greedy for its power.

Therefore, margin trading should be done in a calculated way. Traders should keep an account of how many trades they have done in a single session and how much loss or profits they have made.

Margin facility is good for those traders who have strict rules for money management and control over their trading habits. By trading carefully, they can increase their profits with just a small investment. Trading on margin increases a trader's trading power because with the help of margin they can trade for a greater amount than the money in their trading accounts will allow. If your brokerage firm offers merging facility for day trading, consider and plan carefully how you will use it before taking any decision.

In margin trading, all open positions are squared off before markets close for that session and traders are not allowed to carry forward positions that have been opened using the margin facility.

Manage Market Risk

When people think of day trading, they only think of potential profits, not losses. Therefore, day trading attracts so many people that don't see the risk of losses. In stock markets, various events can trigger losses for investors and traders, which are beyond their control. These events can be economic conditions such as recession, geopolitical changes, changes in the central bank policies, natural disasters, or sometimes terror attacks.

This is the market risk; the potential of losing money due to unknown and sudden factors. These factors affect the overall performance of stock markets, and regardless of how careful one is while day trading, the possibility of market risk is always present, which can cause losses. The market risk is known as the systematic risk because it influences the entire stock market. There is also a nonsystematic risk, which affects only a specific industry or company. Long-term investors tackle this risk by diversification in their investment portfolio.

Unlike investors, day traders have no method to neutralize market risk, but they can avoid it by keeping track of financial and business events, news, and economic calendars. For example, stock markets are very sensitive to the central banks' rate policies and become highly volatile on those days. Nobody knows what kind of policy any central bank will adopt in its monetary meeting. But day traders can check the economic calendar and know which day these meetings will take place. They can avoid trading on those days and reduce the risk of loss in trading.

Therefore, knowledge of stock markets and being aware of what is happening in the financial world is essential for day traders. Many successful traders have a policy of staying away from trading on days when any major economic event will take place, or a major decision will be announced. For example, on the day when the result of an important election is declared; any big company's court case decision comes in, or a central banks' policy meeting takes place. On such days, speculative trading dominates stock markets and market risk is very high. Similarly, on a day when any company announces earnings results, its stock price fluctuates wildly, increasing the market risk in trading of that stock.

For inexperienced day traders, the best way to tackle market risk is to avoid trading on such days.

Risk Management Techniques

In day trading, there is always a risk that you will lose money. Now, if you want to start day trading as a career, learn a few techniques that will reduce and manage the risk of potential losses. By taking steps to manage the risk, you reduce the potential day trading losses.

To stay in the day trading business for the long term, you must protect your trading capital. By reducing the risk of losses, you open the possibilities of future profits and a sustainable day trading business.

If you plan well, prepare your trading strategies before starting to trade; you increase the possibility of a stable trading practice which can lead to profits. Therefore, it is essential to prepare your trading plans every day, create trading strategies and follow your trading rules. These three things can make or break your day trading business. Professional day traders always plan their trades first and then trade their plans. This can be understood by an example of two imaginary traders. Suppose there are two traders, trading in the same stock market, trading the same stock. One of them has prepared his trading plan and knows when and how he will trade. The other trader has done no planning and is just sitting there, taking the on-the-spot decisions for buying or selling the stock. Who do you think will be more successful? The one who is well prepared, or the one who has no inkling of what he will do the next second?

The second risk management technique is using stop orders. Use these orders to decide to fix your stop -loss and profit booking points, which will take emotions out of your decision-making process, and automatically cut the losses or book the profit for you.

Many a time, profitable trade turns into loss-making because markets change their trend, but traders do not exit their positions, hoping to increase profits. Therefore, it is necessary to keep a profit booking point and exit the profitable trades at that point. Keeping a fix profit booking point can also help you calculate your returns with every trade and help you avoid taking the unnecessary risk for further trades.

Taking emotions out of day trading is a very important requirement for profitable trading. Do not prejudge the trend in stock markets, which many day traders do and trade against markets, ending with losses.

Using Risk-Reward Ratio

Day trading is done for financial rewards and the good thing is, you can always calculate how much risk you take on every trade and how much reward you can expect. The risk-reward ratio represents the expected reward and expected risk traders can earn on the investment of every dollar.

The risk-reward ratio can excellently indicate your potential profits and potential loss, which can help you in managing your investment capital. For example, a trade with the risk-reward ratio of 1:4 shows that at the risk of $1, the trade has the potential of returning $4. Professional traders advise not to take any trade which has a risk-reward ratio lower than 1:3. This indicates, the trader can expect the investment to be $1, and the potential profit $3.

Expert traders use this method for planning which trade will be more profitable and take only those trades. Technical charting is a good technique to decide the risk-reward ratio of any trade by plotting the price moment from support to resistance levels. For example, if a stock has a support level at $20, it will probably rise from that level because many traders are likely to buy it at support levels. After finding out a potential support level, traders try to spot the nearby resistance level where the rising price is expected to pause. Suppose a technical level is appearing at $60. So, the trader can buy at $20 and exit when the price reaches $60. If everything goes right, he can risk $20 to reap a reward of $60. In this trade, the risk-reward ratio will be 1:3.

By calculating the risk-reward ratio, traders can plan how much money they will need to invest, and how much reward they can expect to gain from any trade. This makes them cautious about money management and risk management.

Some traders have a flexible risk-reward ratio for trading, while others prefer to take trades only with a fixed risk-reward ratio. Keeping stop-loss in all trades also helps in managing the risk-reward ratio. Traders can calculate their trade entry point to stop-loss as the risk, and trade entry to profit as the reward. This way, they can find out if any trade has a bigger risk than the potential reward or a bigger reward than the potential risk. Choosing trades with bigger profits and smaller risks can increase the amount of profit over a period.

Overview

Without learning money management, all your knowledge about stock and day trading is useless. If you don't use effective techniques for managing your investment, then you may soon find your money running out and you will have to shut down your day trading business. There are various methods for money management in intraday trading. It will be a good idea to learn a few techniques for it and it and strictly apply those rules to your trading business. Keeping the trading cost to a minimum and putting stop-loss in all trades are effective money management tricks.

Margin trading facilities are given for day trading and can be used astutely for increasing profits. At the same time, margin facilities can make day traders greedy, make them commit the mistake of over-trading, and incurring losses. Margin facility is borrowing money from your brokerage firm and trading on borrowed money is never a good idea. It is better to avoid margin trading until you have enough experience in stock markets and can handle your emotions while trading.

Day trading is not only profitable but can always lead to losses because of the ever-present market risk. Various events can trigger this risk and affect the performance of the overall stock markets. Day traders have no control over it. However, many strategies can help day traders avoid market risk, and reduce the potential loss that it can cause. Knowledge of stock markets' functioning and checking economic calendars can help day traders avoid some market risks.

Traders always face the risk of financial loss. Therefore, they must use strategies for risk management in day trading. Protecting your trading capital should be your first aim so you can stay in the day trading business for the long term. Creating trading plans and trading strategies are steps that can help traders avoid loss-making trades. Using stop orders is another method that can help traders reduce the losses and book their profits at the right time.

Calculating the risk-reward ratio is another method for money management and reducing risk trading. Traders can calculate how much risk a trade carries and how much potential profit it can earn for them. They can choose only those trades that carry a bigger reward and smaller risk and thus earn more profits in the long-term. Some professional traders prefer to trade only when the rewards are much higher than the potential risk.

CHAPTER 8:
Trading Psychology: An Important Factor

To succeed in day trading, day traders require many skills, including the ability to analyze a technical chart. But none of the technical skills can replace the importance of a traders' mind-set. Discipline, quick thinking, and emotional control; all these are collectively called the trading psychology and are important factors for succeeding in the day trading business.

On the surface, day trading is an easy activity; markets go up and down and traders buy and sell with the price. Then how come 90% of traders make losses in day trading? The answer lies in trading psychology where most of the day traders fail. You will see many online courses advertising to teach day trading or technical analysis, but It is unheard of any course that teaching trading psychology to traders.

It is a well-known fact that controlling emotions of fear and greed are two of the most difficult decisions a day trader can take. Even those who prepare a trading plan, create trading rules; find it hard to stick to those rules and plans while trading in the stock markets. It is like dieting. When you are not supposed to think of ice cream, all you can do is think of ice cream.

Nobody is born with a successful trader's mindset. it is a skill developed with practice and self-discipline. Humans are emotional beings, so it is difficult to take emotions completely out of day trading. But traders can try to remain neutral and take the help of technology to trade, so their decisions are based on facts.

It is so easy to look at a chart and point, what was a good buying point and how much profit one could have made by trading in a certain way. But once markets open and the stock price starts changing its tracks, it sorts of hypnotizes traders in making wrong decisions. Emotions like greed and fear take over and traders keep making mistakes, accumulating losses instead of what should have been easy profits.

In stock markets, the simplest thing is the stock price's movement. It keeps going up or down rhythmically. Any child can tell when the price is going down, or when the price is going up. Still, day traders make the mistake of buying when the price is falling and selling when the price is rising. At any given time, half of the day traders believe that markets are at a good point to buy stocks, and the other half of day traders firmly believe that it is the right time to sell. Some of these traders are right half of the time, and some of these traders are wrong half of the time. Overall, none of them are right all the time. They get confused, not by the price movement; but by their own psychological reactions.

One can easily master the part which belongs to stock markets and trading, but the other part of day trading, the trading psychology, should also be learned for succeeding in day trading.

Understanding Trading Psychology

What exactly is trading psychology? It identifies traders' mental and emotional state, which contributes to their success or failure in stock trading or trading any other financial security. trading psychology is more important in day trading because here, traders must decide quickly and get to trade only for a few hours. It is like being boxed a small timeframe. For example, if a person is given two things to choose from, and given a time limit of 3 hours, he will do it in a relaxed way. However, if he is asked to decide within 3 seconds, he will panic. In other words, he will get into an emotional state.

Trading psychology involves two aspects; risk-taking and self-discipline. Traders know that emotions like greed and fear should not influence them, but they allow these emotions to affect their trading. Two other emotions are equally destructive; namely, hope and regret. Anger is an emotion that causes considerable loss to traders when they get frustrated by failure and indulge in revenge trading; which leads to more losses.

In greed, traders take more risk than is safe for them. In fear, traders avoid risk and generate very small profits.

Greed can encourage traders to indulge in over-trading. At times, it can cloud their rational thinking and judgment. It can lead to behavior that cannot be explained rationally. Traders may try to place big trades in a hurry to earn profits. If their trades are profitable, they may refuse to exit these trades even if the exit point has come and continue holding positions hoping for bigger profits. This behavior ultimately ends with loss because markets do not keep trending in one direction. Eventually, the market trend changes, and the profitable position turn into a loss-making one.

Fear has the opposite effect but the same result for traders. In the grip of fear, traders may close their position prematurely, then trade again to earn profits. It becomes a vicious cycle of fear and greed, where the trader is afraid to keep the position open longer but keeps trading again in greed. This results in over trading and losses. Fear is the hallmark of a bear market, where price tumbles down rapidly when panicky traders try to get out of their positions. Similarly, greed dominates the bull market, where traders take unnecessary risks and blindly buy stocks or other securities, hoping for making quick profits. The Dot-com bubble was a classic example of greed in stock markets, and the Dot-com bubble burst was a classic example of fear in stock markets when prices crashed rapidly.

Fear and Day Trading

The technical progress has made it possible for news to travel quick and reach far-flung places. This has created a unique situation for stock markets, where the positive news has a quick and positive reaction in the stock markets; but negative news causes sudden and a steep drop in stock prices as traders become gripped by fear and panic.

In situations leading to greed, traders still pause and think, if they are being greedy. But under the influence of fear, traders usually overreact and exit their position quickly. This has a chain-reaction effect on markets. Prices fall, traders sell in fear; prices fall further, traders sell more in fear. This emotion creates bigger ripples in stock markets than greed. Traders exit from their positions fearing that they will lose their profits or make losses. The fear of loss paralyzes novice traders when their positions turn into loss-making. They refuse to exit such positions, hoping for a bounce-back in markets, hoping to turn their losses into profits. What should have been a small loss, eventually turns into a big one for them, sometimes even wiping out their all trading capital. A rationally thinking person will quickly exit from such a position. But fear is such strong emotion in day trading, that it stops even rational people from taking correct decisions.

Technology can help traders make the right decision in such situations. Automated trading is one aspect of trading that eliminates emotional content from day trading. But automated trading software is expensive and not every trader can afford those. So, the next best thing is to take the help of stop and limit orders. Based on your trading plan, decide what will be your trade entry, exit, stop loss and profit booking levels. To stop yourself from trading before the trade entry point has arrived, put a limit order for that level. It will free you from watching the price constantly. And, if you are not watching markets constantly, the chance of wrong trading is also removed.

You cannot remove emotions from life. Therefore, it will remain a part of your day trading business. But you can control it by self-discipline and proper trade management techniques. Patience is also one such technique, where you stay away from trading until the right trade entry level arrives.

Greed, Another Enemy

Greed leads people to day trading, and greed leads them to losses in stock markets. Traders who are earning $1 in profit, become greedy and want to make a profit of $3. After reaching that level, they want it to reach $30. In the end, they exit with losses instead of any profit at all. Greed takes away their profits and hands them losses instead. There is another way greed makes day traders accumulate losses even after making a profit. Once a trader makes some profit, he thinks, the next trade will also bring him profits. So, he trades again. And again, and again. By the end of the session, profits disappear, and losses remain. Then regret takes over; if only he had stopped trading after the first profitable trade. This same cycle is repeated day after day. Greed and regret come hand in hand in the stock trading business.

Greed is the most difficult emotion to overcome in stock trading. The lure of easy money, of quick profits, is very difficult to resist. But, like fear, traders can overcome greed by developing a trading plan and following it is strictly. When a trade is earning profits, it is difficult to exit it at the profit booking level. The simple method to get over this greed is to put a stop order to exit the trade at the pre-planned level.

Over-trading is a loss-making result of greed. Traders keep buying and selling without realizing how many times they have traded, or how much loss they have accumulated. To avoid this trap, trade only a few times in a day, keep this number to a minimum and stop trading ones that limit is reached. Exit the market and do not look back. If you think, "I will not trade, but there is no harm looking at the markets", you will be unable to resist the temptation of trading just one more time. That one trade will start a series of wrong trades and over-trading. Self-control and discipline are as much required in day trading, like any other skill. Day trading tests traders' mental strength and emotional control. It may take time to develop these skills but following your rules can help eliminate mistakes from your trading. If you reduce your loss-making habits, the chances of your profitability will increase dramatically.

Rule-Based Trading

To protect yourself from psychological risks in day trading, you must take steps to eliminate this before you start trading. There is only one thing that can protect you from the emotional rollercoaster ride in stock markets, which is a ruled based trading system.

All aspects of your day trading must be governed by a set of rules, which will involve your trading plan and trading strategies. Every day, you must go over these rules and trade accordingly.

Before you trade, sit down and think, why you will start day trading? Are you going to do it for a side income? Are you going to do it for the excitement of stock markets? Or, are you going to do it to prove any point to somebody? Many traders fall into the egotistical trap of proving themselves right in trading. They will keep trading against the market and expect the market to change its course, instead of changing their trading style.

If you are starting day trading to earn a living, then this thought should always be uppermost in your mind. You cannot allow yourself to be distracted by small profits and losses and trade indiscriminately. This should be your goal, to earn a living, and it should be your aim of day trading every day. Before you trade, remind yourself that you are doing this for a living, not for the short-term excitement. Therefore, if you make any loss, remind yourself that in business, difficulties are a part of the cycle. Try to maintain a neutral mental state whether you make profits and losses. All your trades must be done according to your plans and strategy. Before you take any trade, know the risk-reward ratio; why you enter that trade; and when you will exit the trade with a profit or at a stop loss.

Create rules about:

1. How many trades you will make every day?

2. What will be your loss tolerance limit for a single session?

3. What will be your profit target for one session?

Stop trading when any of these three criteria are completed. For example, if you decided to take only two trades in a session, stop trading for that session once you have completed your two trades, whether your trades were profitable. If you have created a threshold of $20 loss for a single station, stop trading if you have reached that loss limit for the session. This will teach you disciplined trading, and you will consciously try to keep your losses to a minimum.

A similar rule should be applied for profit booking. Stop trading for the day if you have reached the profit target. This profit target could be in terms of a fixed amount, or the number of successful trades. For example, some traders stop trading once they have made a profitable trade. This is one of the best greed management techniques. If you have made a profit in stock trading, even if it is tiny, just pocket it and run away from markets. Otherwise, greed will take over and you will over-trade, trying to make more profit, and end up with losses.

Why Trading Psychology is Important

Most of the people fail in day trading because they start at the wrong end. They start by learning trading skills first, then move on to money and risk management techniques, and the last stop is to learn, superficially, about trading psychology.

In fact, the right sequence of learning day trading should be learning the trading psychology first, then money and risk management techniques and the last part should constitute learning the trading skills. It is very easy to learn technical analysis and how to use technical indicators. But it is very difficult to control one's emotions like fear and greed while trading, or astutely manage money while day trading.

If you look at people in different fields, you will find the mind-set is the main difference between those who reach the pinnacle of their chosen career and those who remain mediocre. Be it business, science, technology, sports, or any other creative pursuit, people who train their minds for success are the ones who win the race. In intraday trading also, hundreds and thousands of day traders use the same methods of technical analysis, however, only a few of them succeed in making profitable trade and others go home with losses. it is the trading psychology, that makes the difference between successful traders and those who failed.

Every trader, who tries to learn day trading, knows that there are certain rules to be followed and still the majority of them fail to do so find therefore if you want to succeed in day trading, you must pay attention to how you react to markets. stock trading is nothing but watching the price rise and fall and trading off with the trend. But still, traders fail to follow this simple method of trading. Day trading happens 90% in the mind of a day trader, and only 10% in what happens in markets. A day trader takes decision based on what he or she thinks is going to happen in stock markets, and not on what is happening. This is the biggest mistake of day traders do and the reason is their emotions.

To overcome this psychological hurdle, day traders must learn how to manage their trades without emotions. They can do so only with the help of technology, and self-discipline. If they do not have self-control or do not follow a disciplined trading plan, they cannot make profits in stock markets.

Overview

For a successful day trading career, traders need to gain many technical skills, but the most important factor that will impact their success is trading psychology. Humans are emotional beings, and it is a well-known fact that traders fail to control two main emotions: fear and greed, which leads to their failure in day trading. Traders are not born with the mindset necessary for success in day trading. But it is a skill that can be developed over time and with practice.

Trading psychology is related to traders' emotional and mental reactions to how markets trend. Day trading exerts extra pressure on traders because here, traders must make quick decisions. There are two aspects of trading psychology, self-discipline, and risk-taking. Many emotions can cause financial harm to day traders. These are greed, fear, anger, hope, and regret. In a bull market, most traders exhibit greed, and in the bear market, most traders panic and trade under fear.

The psychological factor behind fear in stock trading is traders, being afraid of losing money. Sometimes traders are afraid that they will make a loss in stock trading. This can impact their decision-making ability. In fear, traders can over-trade or not trade even when a profitable opportunity comes in stock markets. Technology can help traders overcome their fearful mindset. By using stop orders and limit orders, traders can take the emotion out of their trading.

Like fear, greed is another enemy of the day trader. Greed is the emotion that leads people to day trading, and the same emotion leads them to financial losses in this field. It is very difficult to resist the temptation of quick profits in stock markets. Traders can overcome greed by creating a trading plan and sticking to the trading rules. Day trading requires mental strength and emotional control. Both can be developed with disciplined trading.

An effective method to overcome the obstacle of trading psychology is rule-based trading. Traders should make rules for every aspect of their day trading business. They should plan and create trading strategies, then strictly follow these. They should decide the number of trades, where to put stop-loss, and decide their profit booking level, then every day, trade according to these fixed numbers. Following these decisions will teach them self-discipline and protect them from the pitfalls of emotional trading.

Day Trading Glossary

Some common trading terms you will come across while day trading.

A

Ask

Ask price is what a seller offers to a buyer, for selling any financial asset.

B

Broker

A broker can be an individual or a firm that acts as an intermediary between traders and exchanges and receives a commission whenever a trade is executed between these two parties.

Bid

In day trading bid price is what a buyer offers to a seller, for purchasing any financial asset.

Bear

Traders who have a negative outlook on markets, and expect the price to fall, are called bears.

Bear Market

In a bear or a bearish market, the price trend continuously declines.

Bull

Traders who have a positive outlook on the market, and expect the price to rise, are nicknamed bulls.

Bull Market

Markets with the rising price pattern are called a Bull market.

C

Cash Market

A market where actual stocks and commodities are traded.

Call Option

Options contracts that are bullish on markets. Popular among day traders.

D

Daily Trading Limit

Exchanges set the maximum price range each day for any contract. The daily trading limit does not mean that it will halt the trading, but only places a limit on the movement of price.

Day Order

An order placed during an intraday session, valid only for that session. It automatically gets canceled when the session closes.

Day Trade

Buying and selling of financial assets on the same day. These assets can be stocks, commodities, forex, or options.

Day Traders

Traders who buy or sell financial assets through a single session and close all their positions before the end of the day. They do not carry forward their positions for the next session.

E

Exchange

A regulated, central marketplace where buyers and sellers trade financial assets.

F

Futures

Derivative contracts that cover the buying and selling of financial assets for future delivery. These trades take place on a futures exchange.

Futures Contract

These are derivative agreements conducted through a futures exchange. These are legally binding on traders who buy or sell financial instruments for future delivery. Futures contracts have standard regulations based on quantity and delivery time.

G

Good till Canceled (GTC)

Open orders with buying or selling instructions at a specific future price and can remain open till the order is executed.

H

Hedge

The simultaneous buying and selling of a derivative contract of a later date. This is done to balance a loss and profit of open positions in derivatives and cash markets.

Hedger

When companies or individuals, who are holding positions in cash markets, do an opposite trade in the derivatives markets to balance any potential loss, they are called hedgers.

Hedging

The act of balancing any potential risk of loss in cash markets by taking an equal, but opposite position in the derivative markets.

I

Initial Margin

To open a new position in derivative markets; such as in futures and options, traders are required to deposit a minimum amount of money in their trading accounts, called initial margin. This is to mitigate any risk of loss because of market volatility. The level of initial margin can increase or decrease according to the market volatility.

L

Last Trading Day

The last trading day is not the last day of the month but the last trading day of derivative contracts (futures & options). On this trading day, the monthly derivative contracts are settled among traders.

Limit Order

An order, given to buy or sell a financial instrument at a specific price, beyond which the order is not filled. This shows that the buyer or seller will trade only at a specific price.

Liquidity

A characteristic of tradable financial instruments, which shows the ease of trading those. Traders and investors prefer to buy or sell highly liquid assets because these can be easily bought or sold.

Long

A trader is supposed to be 'long' if he has a bullish outlook for the market. A long position is taken when buyers expect the price to rise.

M

Maintenance Margin

This is the minimum value traders must keep in their trading account if they wish to keep a position open. The maintenance margin is usually lower compared to the initial margin.

Margin Call

If a trader's account falls short of required maintenance margin, they receive a call from the brokerage firm, demanding to deposit the required amount. If a trader does not do so, the brokerage firm liquidates his positions amounting to the same value.

Market Order

An order to buy or sell any financial entity at the latest available price. Traders use this order when they want their trades to be executed quickly.

Market on Close

This order is used to buy or sell financial assets at the end of that trading session. The order price is typically within the closing range of market prices.

O

Offer Price

It shows the willingness of the seller to sell a financial asset at an agreed price. It is also called 'Ask' price.

Open Order

An order which is not executed. It can remain open till the specified price is reached, or the order is canceled.

P

Pit

A specific place on the trading floor where traders conduct their buying and selling activities.

Position

A trade that has not been completed the process of both buying and selling. An open trade.

S

Settlement Price

This is the last price paid for any financial entity on a trading day. This is also called the closing price.

Scalp

A day trading method, where speculators trade for small profits. These trades are completed very quickly, within a few minutes. Scalpers trade multiple times through the same day.

Short

When a trader has a negative or bearish outlook on the market, he is said to be short on the market. Also, the selling side of an open derivative contract.

Speculator

Traders who try to anticipate market movements and price changes, to earn profits.

Spot

Markets, where immediate delivery and cash payment is handled for financial assets.

Spread

Difference between the bid and ask price.

Stop Order

Also known as the stop-loss order. Traders use this order to limit the risk of loss or book profits at a certain price level.

Stop Limit

Like a stop order, but with a slight variation. Stop order with limit acts as a limit order in buying when the price is at or above the stop price. In selling, it becomes a limit order when the price is trading at or below the stock price.

T

Tick

In trading, the smallest increment in the price of any financial asset. Some scalpers use tick price for trading.

.